Global Labour and the Migrant Premium

This book provides the first systematic account of the premium costs that migrants pay to live and work abroad.

Reducing the costs of international labour migration, specifically worker-paid costs for low-skilled employment, has become an important item on the global agenda over the last years and is particularly pertinent for the UN's Global Compact on Safe, Orderly and Regular Migration. Recruitment costs alone amount in most migration corridors to anywhere between one and ten months of foreign earnings and many migrants may well lose between one and two years of foreign earnings, if all costs are considered. This book is intended as a primer for evidence-based policy for reducing the costs of international labour mobility. The contributors include academics from law, economics and politics, but also authors from international organizations and non-governmental organizations, as well as the voices of migrants. The hope of the editors is that this small collection sets the basis for evidence-based policies that seek to reduce the costs of international migration.

This book will be of interest to scholars and students of migration, globalization, law, sociology and international relations, as well as practitioners and policy makers.

Tugba Basaran is Senior Research Fellow at the Centre for the Study of Global Human Movement, University of Cambridge, UK, and visiting researcher at Harvard Law School. Her publications include *Security, Law and Borders: At the Limits of Liberties* (Routledge, 2011) and *International Political Sociology: Transversal Lines*, co-edited with Didier Bigo, Emmanuel P. Guittet and R. B. J. Walker (Routledge, 2016).

Elspeth Guild is a Jean Monnet Professor ad personam in law at Queen Mary University of London, UK, and Radboud University, Netherlands. She regularly advises EU institutions on migration and asylum-related matters and has written studies for the European Parliament on the European dimension of the refugee crisis in 2016. Her publications include *Security and Migration in the 21st Century* (2009) and *The Human Rights of Migrants in the 21st Century*, co-edited with Stefanie Grant and Kees Groenendijk (Routledge, 2017).

Routledge Studies in Liberty and Security
Series editors: Didier Bigo, Elspeth Guild, R. B. J. Walker and Tugba Basaran

This book series will establish connections between critical security studies and International Relations, surveillance studies, criminology, law and human rights, political sociology and political theory. To analyse the boundaries of the concepts of liberty and security, the practices which are enacted in their name (often the same practices) will be at the heart of the series. These investigations address contemporary questions informed by history, political theory and a sense of what constitutes the contemporary international order.

Security and Defensive Democracy in Israel
A Critical Approach to Political Discourse
Sharon Weinblum

Managing State Fragility
Conflict, Quantification, and Power
Isabel Rocha de Siqueira

Governing Diasporas in International Relations
The Transnational Politics of Croatia and Former Yugoslavia
Francesco Ragazzi

Human Rights of Migrants in the 21st Century
Edited by Elspeth Guild, Stefanie Grant and C. A. Groenendijk

Global Labour and the Migrant Premium
The Cost of Working Abroad
Edited by Tugba Basaran and Elspeth Guild

For more information about this series, please visit: www.routledge.com/Routledge-Studies-in-Liberty-and-Security/book-series/RSLS

Global Labour and the Migrant Premium

The Cost of Working Abroad

Edited by Tugba Basaran and Elspeth Guild

Routledge
Taylor & Francis Group
LONDON AND NEW YORK

First published 2019
by Routledge
2 Park Square, Milton Park, Abingdon, Oxon OX14 4RN

and by Routledge
711 Third Avenue, New York, NY 10017

Routledge is an imprint of the Taylor & Francis Group, an informa business

British Library Cataloguing-in-Publication Data
A catalogue record for this book is available from the British Library

Library of Congress Cataloging-in-Publication Data
Names: Basaran, Tugba, editor. | Guild, Elspeth, editor.
Title: Global labour and the migrant premium : the cost of working abroad / edited by Tugba Basaran and Elspeth Guild.
Description: Abingdon, Oxon ; New York, NY : Routledge, 2019. | Series: Routledge studies in liberty and security | Includes bibliographical references and index.
Identifiers: LCCN 2018019311| ISBN 9781138606999 (hardback) | ISBN 9780429467387 (e-book)
Subjects: LCSH: Foreign workers. | Labor market. | Emigration and immigration–Economic aspects.
Classification: LCC HD6300 .G56 2019 | DDC 331.5/44–dc23
LC record available at https://lccn.loc.gov/2018019311

ISBN: 978-1-138-60699-9 (hbk)
ISBN: 978-0-429-46738-7 (ebk)

Typeset in Times New Roman
by Wearset Ltd, Boldon, Tyne and Wear

Contents

Illustrations

Figures

Table

Contributors

Anthony Amicelle is Associate Professor in Criminology at the Université de Montréal and regular researcher at the Montreal Centre for International Studies (CERIUM) and the International Centre for Comparative Criminology (ICCC). His research examines practices of policing, surveillance and intelligence at the interface of finance and security, especially with respect to counter-terrorism and anti-money laundering. His recent publications include (with Vanessa Iafolla) "Suspicion-in-the-Making: Surveillance and Denunciation in Financial Policing" (*British Journal of Criminology*, 2017) and "Policing through Misunderstanding: Insights from the Configuration of Financial Policing" (*Crime, Law and Social Change*, 2017).

Idil Atak is an Associate Professor and the Graduate Program Director in the Department of Criminology of Ryerson University. She received her PhD from the Université de Montréal's Faculty of Law. Idil is a member of the International Association for the Study of Forced Migration's (IASFM) Executive Committee, the past president of the Canadian Association for Refugee and Forced Migration Studies (CARFMS) and a research associate at Hans and Tamar Oppenheimer Chair in Public International Law of McGill University. She is currently conducting a Social Sciences and Humanities Research Council of Canada (SSHRC)-funded research on the intersection of security, irregular migration and asylum.

Tugba Basaran is Senior Research Fellow at the Centre for the Study of Global Human Movement, University of Cambridge and visiting researcher at Harvard Law School. She holds a PhD from the University of Cambridge, and has worked as assistant professor at the University of Kent. Her publications include *Security, Law and Borders: At the Limits of Liberties* (2011) and the co-edited volume *International Political Sociology: Transversal Lines* (2016). Prior to her academic career, Tugba Basaran worked for many years in international relations and international development, amongst others, in El Salvador, Haiti, the Philippines, Bosnia and Herzegovina, and Kosovo.

Julinda Beqiraj is Associate Senior Research Fellow at the Bingham Centre for the Rule of Law (British Institute of International and Comparative Law – BIICL). She holds a PhD from the University of Trento (Italy) and her doctoral dissertation focused on the international protection of the economic and social rights of migrant workers. At the Bingham Centre she works on a number of projects, including on the role of the rule of law in the context of the 2030 Sustainable Development Goals, and on barriers and solutions to access to justice across jurisdictions.

Jacqueline Bhabha, JD, MsC, is Professor of the Practice of Health and Human Rights at the Harvard T.H. Chan School of Public Health and Director of Research at the Harvard FXB Center for Health and Human Rights. From 1997 to 2001, Bhabha directed the Human Rights Programme at the University of Chicago. Prior to 1997 she was a practising human rights lawyer in London and at the European Court of Human Rights in Strasbourg. She has published extensively on issues of transnational child migration, refugee protection, children's rights and citizenship. Professor Bhabha currently serves on the board of the Scholars at Risk Network, the World Peace Foundation, the Institute on Statelessness and Inclusion, and the *Journal of Refugee Studies*. She is a frequent adviser to UNHCR, UNICEF, IOM and civil society organizations working on forced migration-related issues.

Ryszard Cholewinski is the Senior Migration Specialist in the ILO Regional Office for Arab States in Beirut. Previously, he was a Migration Policy Specialist at ILO in Geneva. Prior to joining the ILO in September 2010, he was a Senior Migration Policy and Research Specialist at the IOM in Geneva and Reader in Law at the University of Leicester in the United Kingdom. He is a lawyer by training with 13 years of previous experience in an academic setting. He has written widely on international labour migration, the human rights of migrants and various aspects of European law and policy relating to migration and asylum.

Craig Churchill is the Chief of the Social Finance Programme and the Team Leader of the ILO's Impact Insurance Facility. He has more than two decades of microfinance experience in both developed and developing countries. In his current position as the chief of the ILO's Social Finance Programme, he focuses on the potential of financial services and policies to achieve social objectives. He serves on the governing board of the Access to Insurance Initiative and was the founding Chair of the Microinsurance Network. He has authored and edited over 40 articles, papers, monographs and training manuals on various microfinance topics, including microinsurance, customer loyalty, organizational development, governance, lending methodologies, regulation and supervision, and financial services for the poorest of the poor.

François Crépeau, OC, is Full Professor and holds the Hans and Tamar Oppenheimer Chair in Public International Law, at the Faculty of Law of McGill University. He was the United Nations Special Rapporteur on the Human Rights of Migrants from 2011 to 2017. He is a fellow of the Royal Society of Canada. In August 2015, he became Director of McGill's Centre for Human Rights and Legal Pluralism. He was appointed to Belgium's International Francqui Professor Chair in Social Sciences for 2017–2018. François Crépeau was 2016 Robert F. Drinan Visiting Professor of Human Rights, Georgetown University. The focus of his current research includes migration control mechanisms, the rights of foreigners, the interface between security and migration, and the interface between the Rule of Law and globalization.

Aparna Dalal is a Senior Research Officer at the ILO's Impact Insurance Facility. She leads the Facility's Research and Innovation initiative that supports practitioners to develop valuable risk management solutions for low-income and emerging customers. She has a decade of technology and business management experience in the public and private sector. Before joining the ILO, Aparna was the Director of Special Projects at the Financial Access Initiative at New York University, where she led microinsurance research projects.

Rudi Fortson QC has been a barrister in independent private practice for some 40 years specializing in transnational crime, and a Visiting Professor of Law at Queen Mary University of London. He has written and lectured extensively on UK (and overseas) criminal law issues.

Bjarney Friðriksdóttir defended her PhD thesis "What Happened to Equality? The Construction of the Right to Equal Treatment in European Union Law on Labour Migration" at Radboud University in November 2016. She holds a Master degree in International Affairs and a Master in European and International Law. Her work experience includes advising a task force on trafficking in human beings at the Council of the Baltic Sea States, working with international organizations such as UNHCR and UN WOMEN, in the field for several years and as the Director of the Icelandic Human Rights Centre. Currently she works as a human rights officer on people on the move for the OHCHR regional office for the Middle East and North Africa.

Gan is an international labour migrant from Thailand. He worked in the construction industry in Saudi Arabia in the 1980s before moving to the UK, where he worked largely in the hotel and catering industries.

Elspeth Guild is a Jean Monnet Professor ad personam in law at Queen Mary University of London and Radboud University, Nijmegen, Netherlands. She regularly advises EU institutions on migration and asylum-related matters and has written studies for the European Parliament on the European dimension of the refugee crisis in 2016. She also advises the Council of Europe and has written two Issue Papers for the Council of Europe Commissioner for Human Rights, one on the right to leave a country, the other on criminalization of migration. Her monograph is particularly relevant: *Security and Migration in the 21st Century* (Polity, Cambridge, 2009). In 2017, she co-edited, with Stefanie Grant and Kees Groenendijk, *The Human Rights of Migrants in the 21st Century*, published by Routledge for the Focus series.

Bethany Hastie is an Assistant Professor at the Peter A. Allard School of Law, University of British Columbia. She completed her law degree (JD) at the University of British Columbia, and her Master of Laws (LLM) and Doctorate in Law (DCL) at McGill University.

Martin O. Heisler, Professor Emeritus of Government and Politics at the University of Maryland, from the small town of Szabadszállás in Hungary, became a refugee in Austria and France after World War II, immigrating to the United States at age 12. After earning a PhD in Political Science and International Relations at the University of California, Los Angeles, he taught at the University of Maryland, Aarhus University and, as a Visiting Professor, Sciences Po in Paris. He held fellowships at CNRS, the University of Warwick, Brussels and elsewhere, publishing on migration, ethnic relations and international security in numerous books and scholarly journals on both sides of the Atlantic.

Yewa S. Holiday is a Lecturer in Criminal Justice at the School of Law and the Institute of Policing at the University of Chester, UK. Her doctorate at Queen Mary University of London examined the criminalization of refugees in England and Wales in the context of article 31(1) of the 1951 Refugee Convention. Prior to her PhD, she worked at the Criminal Cases Review Commission in Birmingham, UK, where she reviewed suspected miscarriages of justice.

Valsamis Mitsilegas is Professor of European Criminal Law and Global Security, Academic Lead for Internationalization and, since 2012, Head of the Department of Law at Queen Mary University of London (QMUL). He served as Dean for Research for the Humanities and Social Sciences and Inaugural Director of the Queen Mary Institute for the Humanities and Social Sciences (IHSS) from January to December 2017 and has been the Director of the Queen Mary Criminal Justice Centre since 2011. From 2001 to 2005, he served as legal adviser to the House of Lords European Union Committee. His research interests and expertise lie in the fields of European criminal law; migration, asylum and borders; security and human rights, including the impact of mass surveillance on privacy; and legal responses to transnational crime, including organized crime and money laundering. He is the author of six monographs and over 100 articles and chapters in academic volumes. His latest books are *The Criminalisation of Migration in Europe* (2015) and *EU Criminal Law After Lisbon* (2016).

Dilip Ratha is Head of KNOMAD and Lead Economist, Migration and Remittances, at the World Bank. Mr Ratha is currently working to lower remittance fees and provide innovative financing solutions for people, businesses and governments. He has worked extensively on migration and innovative financing for development, including remittances, diaspora bonds and prediction of sovereign credit ratings. His TED Talk, "The hidden force in global economics: sending money home", has had 1.3 million views. He is the founder of KNOMAD, co-founder of Migrating Out of Poverty Research Consortium and the brain behind Africa Institute for Remittances.

Ganesh Seshan is a Senior Economist in the Migration and Remittances team at the World Bank and a member of the KNOMAD Secretariat. His research interest is on the economics of developing countries, particularly on migration where the focus is on examining policies and social programmes to enhance the developmental impact of migration and remittances. This includes the use of financial education, skills training and information campaigns. Seshan's research has been published, among others, in the *Journal of Development Economics*, *World Bank Economic Review*, *Oxford Economic Papers* and the *Journal of Development Studies*.

Alyna C. Smith is Advocacy Officer at PICUM, where she leads their work on access to health care and access to justice. Before joining PICUM, she was a litigation associate at a global law firm in New York where she developed an extensive pro bono practice in the areas of where she developed an extensive pro bono practice in the areas of criminal justice, immigration law and human rights. Her prior work experience includes a clerkship with Canada's Federal Court, and work on ethics, genetics and access to medicines for the World Health Organization. Alyna holds a bachelor's degree in human biology and ethics, a master's degree in philosophy and a degree in law from the University of Toronto.

Abbreviations

CRC	Convention on the Rights of the Child 1989
Declaration on Human Rights	The Universal Declaration of Human Rights 1948
ECHR	European Convention on Human Rights
GCM	Global Compact on Migration
GCR	Global Compact on Refugees
ICCPR	International Covenant on Civil and Political Rights 1966
ICESCR	International Covenant on Economic, Social and Cultural Rights 1966
ILO	International Labour Organization
IOM	International Organization for Migration
MWC	International Convention on the Protection of the Rights of All Migrant Workers and Members of Their Families 1990
NY Declaration	The New York Declaration of Refugees and Migrants adopted by the General Assembly on 19 September 2016
OHCHR	Office of the UN High Commissioner for Human Rights
Refugee Convention	Convention Relating to the Status of Refugees 1951 and its 1967 Protocol
SDG	UN Sustainable Development Goals

1 The premium

Tugba Basaran and Elspeth Guild

We will commit to reducing the costs of labour migration ...
(New York Declaration for Refugees and Migrants 2016, para 46)

Over previous years, reducing the cost of migration has become central to the global agenda.[1] As high-skilled workers are enticed to cross borders by the promise of higher wages and lofty benefits, low-skilled recruits are considered indefinitely dispensable and bear tremendous costs for working abroad.[2] For low-skilled employment, including domestic, agricultural, factory and construction work, recruitment costs alone can amount to ten months of foreign earnings and many are likely to lose one to two years of foreign earnings, if all worker-borne costs are considered. The poorest and most marginalized often pay the highest premium.[3] This collection provides the first systematic account of costs borne by migrants, that is the *premium* that migrants pay to live and work abroad. In the following, we seek to reveal what these premium costs entail, how they are distributed and who encounters them where.

An inquiry into the migrant premium appears particularly pertinent today. In 2015, an estimated 244 million persons lived in a country other than where they were born, with a large majority moving for purposes of employment.[4] The international community has repeatedly asserted the benefits of international migration, particularly for sustainable development: at more than US$430 billion, recorded remittance flows of migrants and diasporas to developing countries are more than three times the official development assistance and commonly higher and less volatile than foreign direct investments.[5] For many countries, remittances represent the largest source of foreign exchange earnings, and for some even more than one-fourth of their GDP.[6] Migration is increasingly conceived as a (potentially) triple-win situation, beneficial to sending countries, destination countries and the migrants themselves. In spite of the numerous benefits of migration, nonetheless it remains excessively priced for the majority, with workers in low-skilled occupations carrying the highest burden.

In this collection, we focus on the premium that low-skilled migrants are exposed to. Contrary to many other studies, our conceptual framework, the migrant premium, illuminates the core actor, the migrant. It requires data-collection and analysis centred on migrants and their journeys, underlining costs and burdens that they encounter in countries of origin, destination and transit – a holistic analysis of the migrant premium.[7] This collection is intended as a primer for evidence-based policy for reducing costs of international labour mobility.[8] Our contributors include academics from law, economics and politics, but also authors from international organizations, including the United Nations, World Bank, ILO, non-governmental organizations, as well as the voices of migrants. Each contribution provides a short and concise expertise on the migrant premium.

Analysing the premium

So far studies on costs of labour migration have largely focused on up-front financial costs, comparing them with the promise of foreign earning streams at later time periods (returns) in an effort to analyse the micro-level decision making process of individuals and households (Sjaastad 1962).[9] In contrast hereto, in this collection, we investigate all additional costs for international (compared to national) labour throughout the migration cycle. The disparity of costs between national and international workers is calculated as the sum of (a) up-front costs for recruitment, but also (b) differentials in wage, working and social conditions in the destination countries, as well as (c) return costs. We state that there is a significant differential between net foreign earnings and the "take-home pay" received after many years abroad, if all costs are considered. Migrants relinquish a significant share of their foreign earnings during the migration cycle, leaving them with severely diminished returns due to direct and indirect costs (differentials, deductions, portability of contributory schemes). But financial costs are only one set of costs encountered by the migrant. There are also less easily quantifiable burdens, barriers and vulnerabilities that migrants are exposed to, including social, legal and health costs. It is the variety of these migration specific costs and burdens that we refer to as the migrant premium.

It is important to point out that the economic analysis of the premium must be understood in the context and subject to states' obligations under international human rights law. We have looked at that in a sister volume already published, but we would like to reiterate here that international human rights obligations almost without exception apply equally to citizens and migrants.[10] In undertaking international human rights obligations, states commit themselves to a floor of rights applicable to everyone, and below which they must not fall, without risking violation of their international duties. First and foremost among those international human rights obligations is the obligation of non-discrimination (and equal treatment) in the delivery of all human rights. Discrimination against migrants on the basis of their status as non-citizens is subject to two regimes in international human rights law. First, for non-derogable human rights such as the prohibition on torture, discrimination on the basis of status is never lawful. Second, for derogable rights, such as family life, any difference in treatment between citizens and migrants must be justified normally to the standard of necessity in a democratic society. Hence, the migrant premium should not only be considered as an economic transaction cost that needs to be diminished, but also analysed in relation to international legal instruments. The reduction of the migrant premium and associated costs may be, under certain conditions (such as prohibited discrimination), not only a desirable outcome, but an international obligation. The table in this introduction (Table 1.1) anchors the migrant premium firmly within the requirements of international human rights law complemented, where applicable, by other international instruments, such as international labour law, refugee law and the sustainable development agenda.

Lastly, we would like to underline that, while the migrant premium is a universally valid concept, it is important to keep in mind that the premium is exposed to strong contextual fluctuations. It varies widely according to journeys and migration corridors, and determinative factors, such as legal status, the destination country (and even locality), the work sector and family composition, strongly influence the premium. Transaction costs are imposed by political, economic and legal institutions. The premium is extracted by various actors, including the destination state directly (i.e. visas, integration tests, language test), indirectly (such as rendering family reunification difficult) and market costs (i.e. wage differentials and housing prices), including an array of public, semi-public and private actors. Therefore, our starting point of analysis must be the economic lives of migrant workers.

Economic lives

The economic lives of migrant workers and the capital accumulation process are anything but smooth. The wages received by migrant workers need to cover not only their own consumption in the host country, but family consumption at home, and generate a surplus for investment at home: minor investments in a house or in a small business, possibly also for retirement. The aspirations of migrant workers and their families are not much different from those of citizens. These small objectives are put to the test abroad, however, due to the migrant premium. Migrant workers are burdened with additional costs throughout the migration cycle: limited channels for travelling to the host country and finding employment, coupled with high cost for intermediaries, visas and also uncompetitive rates for travel are only the starting point. Living separated from their families requires payment for a second house, food and often also for the care of children as well as grandparents and relatives. After consumption here and there, covering the foreseen and the unforeseen (calamities, sicknesses, funerals), the migrant worker still needs to accumulate investment capital. To send money home, migrant workers will also have to pay for financial services. Many cannot rely on banks, even if they have an account; service to their regions of origin are limited and at fees that can even outbid alternative money transfer services. Of course, this does not yet include the non-quantifiable factors – the mental stress, children growing up without one parent (or sometimes both), the impossibility of caring for grandparents. Then, there are a particular set of costs for returning to the home country: if migrant workers opt to go home after years of service abroad, they have difficulties bringing along their pensions and other benefits acquired in the host country.

And, if life as a regular migrant worker is already harsh and exorbitantly expensive, it is even more so for life as an irregular migrant worker. These workers, with the same objectives and obligations, obtain an even lower wage for the same work, are more dependent upon the goodwill of the employer and have less access to justice and an even higher premium for living in the host country. They are also exposed to the possibility of fines, confiscation orders, expulsion and even higher costs for travel routes, often paid multiple times over the time of service of the irregular migrant worker. Even the hardest working migrant workers have difficulties supporting their basic consumption and that of their family, with only minor, occasional prospects for investments. It is these conditions of international labour migrants, and the causes and effects of the migrant premium, that we intend to reveal in this book. The migrant premium – that is, lower wages and exorbitant additional costs – plague the economic lives of international migrants, making it impossible to accumulate capital at the rate available to domestic workers. Under contemporary conditions of international labour, much effort and money are wasted, which could alternatively be used for remittances, investments, sustainable development or for alternative desires of the migrant worker, their families and relatives.

The premier objective of migration governance, we argue, must be to increase the disposable income of migrants, and more specifically the surplus available for investment. This means opening up the currently narrow possibilities for capital accumulation by diminishing exorbitant costs. Increasing migrant contributions requires making the surplus available to migrant workers and their families and closing down the multiple channels for extracting the premium. Starting from the economic lives of migrants, we believe, provides a holistic analytical perspective for migration governance and is necessary for establishing fair labour and living standards for international migrants.

Methodology

Through this collection, we hope to make the reader aware of the complexity of costs that are inherent to the full migration cycle and continue to burden migrants even upon return. In the following chapters of this book, we elucidate costs incurred by low-skilled migrants.[11] These can be categorized into (for an overview, see Table 1.1): (1) *pre-departure costs*, i.e. transportation costs, visa costs, document fees, health check-ups, fees for labour intermediaries and pre-departure loans; (2) *conditions in the destination country*, i.e. wage differentials between international and national labourers, but also in terms of social security benefits, non-contributory income support and health; and (3) *remittance and return costs*, i.e. remittance costs, portability of social entitlements. Together, they constitute the premium, the additional costs that migrants incur compared to nationals. We have chosen a wide range of subjects and authors to illustrate the migrant premium. Each contribution is short and concise, providing expert engagement with particular costs of the migrant premium across a variety of particular destination contexts. We have chosen the most egregious premium costs, and are aware that many costs, including a number of them listed on Table 1.1, which require further investigation, remain unattended to, but we leave that for further studies.

Chapter outline

The initial chapters underline the crucial relation between law and the premium, and elaborate how legal status is crucial to setting premium rates, and determining economic, political and social transaction costs. **Chapter 2** focuses on two particular forms of legal precocity, temporary foreign worker programmes and undocumented migration, exposing these workers to heightened risk of discrimination, abuse, exploitation and violence and the impediments to their effective protection under the law. **Chapter 3** applies the argument to all migrant workers and underlines how migrant workers in many countries cannot benefit from the full enjoyment of

Table 1.1 The migrant premium.

	Breakdown of costs	*International laws and standards*
PRE-DEPARTURE		
Chapter 4	• Transportation costs • Compliance costs, i.e. visa, permit, health test, notarization, integration • Intermediaries	SDG 10.7.1
CONDITIONS IN DESTINATION COUNTRY		
Wages and work conditions *Chapters 2, 3, 5, 11*	• Wage gap • Right to change employment • Freedom of association • Representation in labour unions	ICESCR, art. 6; see also ICESCR, art. 7; SDG 8.8; ILO Conv. 87, 97 (art. 6), 98, 143, 189; MWC, art. 20, 25, 26, 40, 49, 52
Living standards and health *Chapter 6*	• Occupational hazards • Prevalence of illnesses • Health care coverage • Mental health issues • Housing	ICESCR, art. 12; Convention on the Rights of Persons with Disabilities; MWC, art. 28
Family *Chapter 12*	• Family reunification • Children • Education	ICCPR, art. 17, 23, 24; CRC, art. 10; MWC, art. 14, 29, 30, 44, 50
Contributory schemes *Chapter 7*	• Social security coverage • Unemployment insurance • Market insurance	ICESCR, art. 9; Committee on ICESCR, art. 9, General Comment No. 19; MWC, art. 27, 54
Non-contributory schemes	• Health care • Income support • Childcare support	MWC, art. 43, 45
Access to justice *Chapter 9*	• Access to courts and tribunals • Legal aid and assistance • Suspensive effect of appeals	ICCPR, art. 3, 4, 14, 16; MWC, art. 18, 24, SDG 16
RETURN AND REMITTANCES		
Remittances *Chapter 13*	• Remittance costs	SDG 10.c.; MWC, art. 47
Return	• Portability and export of social security, including pensions and health insurance	MWC, art. 32, 48
Fines, confiscation, expulsion *Chapters 8, 10*	• Losses due to legal status of migrant workers	ICCPR, art. 14, 26; MWC, art. 15

international labour standards and human rights law, applicable to all workers.

The following chapters analyse particular worker-paid premium costs during the migration cycle. We have selected some of the most vital premium costs: **Chapter 4** focuses on recruitment costs, **Chapter 5** on wages and working conditions, **Chapter 6** on health costs, **Chapter 7** on risk and insurance, **Chapter 9** on access to justice and **Chapter 13** on remittance and return. We are well aware that these are not all of the premium costs and we could break down each cost for particular groups (regular and irregular workers, children, agricultural workers), into particular sub-costs as well as particular journeys. Neither do we always operationalize the premium in the same way to account for the variety of costs. Some authors are able to provide us with precise financial costs: the chapter on recruitment costs (Chapter 4), for example, written by economists at the World Bank, uses a recruitment cost indicator, consisting of transportation costs, recruitment agency fees and compliance costs. Other chapters, such as on health costs (Chapter 6) are more difficult to convert into a financial equation, but nonetheless equally important as we seek to understand the additional burden carried by migrant workers, compared to their peers.

To underline the variety of premium costs for different categories of workers, we have also included chapters on particular groups that are exposed to a specific premium, relevant to them. **Chapter 8** focuses on irregular migrants, and the vulnerabilities created due to their criminalization. **Chapter 10** follows in these footsteps and underlines how irregular migrants are exposed to particular costs, namely income, penalties and confiscation regimes. **Chapter 11** engages with migration cycles of agricultural workers, and **Chapter 12** with the distinct vulnerabilities of children and young people.

In the last two chapters, we allow for a more personal approach to the migrant premium, following individual journeys of migrants. **Chapter 14** is an interview with Gan, exploring his travels as a migrant worker from Bangkok via Riyadh to London. **Chapter 15** concludes the book with an autobiographic account of the academic and personal journey of Professor Emeritus Martin Heisler.

Future directions

The New York Declaration for Refugees and Migrants, adopted on 19 September 2016, initiated a process to improve the governance of human mobility under the auspices of the United Nations. It has explicitly stated a global commitment to reducing the costs of labour migration (para 46), an objective underlined in the statements of the World Bank, the International Labour Organization and the Global Forum on Migration and Development, amongst others. In line with the Special Rapporteur on Human Rights of Migrants' proposition on "a human-rights and evidence-based governance framework for international migration and mobility",[12] in this collection we have proposed the migrant premium, a conceptual and operational tool for measuring the cost of migration. The analysis of the premium should be complemented by policy measures to reduce the premium globally. In view of the Global Compact on Migration, an inquiry into the costs of international labour migration seems particularly pertinent today. Therefore, achievable goals, targets and indicators need to be developed and set within a reasonable timeframe to diminish the migrant premium.[13]

Notes

1 UN General Assembly, New York Declaration for Refugees and Migrants, 19 September 2016, A/RES/71/1.

2 The term low-skilled migrant workers is used to indicate the occupation (in destination country) and does not necessarily correlate with the qualification. It refers, for example, to the majority of those employed in agriculture, at construction sites, factory plants or as domestic workers in private homes. See also, Bauman, Zygmunt, *Globalization: The Human Consequences*. New York: Columbia University Press, 1998.

3 On the relation between poverty and premium, see also Mendoza, R. U. "Why do the poor pay more? Exploring the poverty penalty concept". *Journal of International Development*, *23*, 1 (2011): 1–28.

4 There is no consensus on who counts as a migrant. In the absence of a universal definition, "migrant" is a highly contested term in public discourse, laws and data sets. Often "international migrant" refers to foreign-born, foreign nationals or long-term foreign nationals, with the respective criteria being the country of birth, nationality and length of stay. These definitions have significant legal implications, however: foreign-born can be citizens or non-citizens; foreign nationals may have been in the country for a day or all their lives – some may even never have set foot in their country of "origin"; refugees may, or may not, be included under migrants, to suppress or underline the special protection regime, the 1951 Convention Relating to Refugees. In this book, we will follow OHCHR's definition of the "international migrant", widely accepted across international actors, as "any person who is outside a State of which he or she is a citizen or national, or in the case of a stateless person, his or her State of birth or habitual residence" (OHCHR, Recommended Principles and Guidelines on Human Rights at International Borders 2014). This definition operates through a distinction to the citizen or national, and considers all migrants, independent of legal status, length of stay and the reasons for mobility. Included are migrant workers and their families, migrants residing with and without authorization, asylum-seekers and stateless persons, among others, while still recognizing the protection of particular international legal regimes, such as the 1951 Convention Relating to Refugees. The above data are based

on: United Nations, Department of Economic and Social Affairs, Population Division, "International Migration Report 2015: Highlights" (ST/ESA/SER.A/375), 2016. In this report, the data are based on national statistics; data on foreign-born are used for 188 countries; data on foreign citizens for 44 countries; the term "diaspora" is used in this report as correlatory data on country of origin.

5 World Bank Group, *Migration and Remittances Factbook 2016*, Washington DC, 2017.

6 This is particularly the case for Haiti, Liberia, Nepal and Tajikistan.

7 Basaran, T. and Guild, E. "Mobilities, ruptures, transitions", in T. Basaran, D. Bigo, E. P. Guittet and R. B. J. Walker, eds., *International Political Sociology: Transversal Lines*. London: Routledge, 2016.

8 By "labour mobility", we cover, following the language of economists, all forms of labour migration, independent of status, and not a limited definition, often used by states, that distinguishes "labour mobility" for desirable labour migration from undesired forms of migration.

9 Sjaastad, Larry A. "The costs and returns of human migration". *Journal of Political Economy*, *70*, 5(2) (1962): 80–93.

10 Guild, E., Grant, S. and Groenendijk, C. A. (eds.), *Human Rights of Migrants in the 21st Century*. London: Routledge, 2017.

11 In this annex, we follow the migrants' journey from country to destination, setting out the additional costs of the migrant premium. This framework provides an outline of various costs associated with the migrant premium. This is by no means an all-inclusive list. For evidence-based policy making, it would be important to disaggregate data by migration corridors and, where applicable, by migration status, employment sector, gender and other characteristics to calculate the migrant premium.

12 UN General Assembly, Report of the Special Rapporteur on Human Rights of Migrants on a 2035 Agenda for Facilitating Human Mobility, 28 April 2017, A/HRC/35/25: page 4.

13 See hereto also ILO, Promoting Decent Work for Migrant Workers, 13th Coordination Meeting on International Migration, New York, 12–13 February 2015.

2 Legal status and vulnerabilities

Idil Atak and François Crépeau

In a globalizing world, demand for migrant workers has grown, enhanced by the mobility of capital, goods, services and information. A factor of development, globalization has, however, also exacerbated the rising differentials in populations' living standards and the uneven distribution of wealth. Growing social inequality is a major driver of international migration.[1] Mobility is facilitated by diasporas and the 'new migration businesses', such as labour recruiters and remittance agencies.[2] Although there are considerable potential gains from reducing barriers to human mobility, legal migration opportunities remain limited, especially in low-wage sectors.[3] Instead, international labour mobility has been marked by two major trends over the past decades.

The first trend is the rise of precarious legal migration statuses. Indeed, States increasingly implement short-term forms of migration regimes, such as circular migration and temporary foreign worker programmes that explicitly apply reduced rights.[4] Take as an example the substantial increase in the number of temporary foreign workers in Canada since 2000. Low-wage temporary migrant workers comprise the largest share of precarious migrants in Canada, as they generally do not have a pathway to permanent residence and only limited access to socioeconomic rights, including health care and collective bargaining. Many are unable to circulate freely in the labour market.[5]

The second trend is the steady increase of undocumented migration which encompasses movement or activities that occur outside of a State's regulatory frameworks. According to the International Labour Organization, globally, some 15 per cent of international migrant workers are in undocumented situations, i.e. without legal authorization for residence and/or employment.[6]

In both cases, the precariousness in which migrant workers find themselves is legally, socially and economically constructed. The causes of undocumented migration are related to 'structural determinants in both sending and receiving countries'.[7] In other words, mobility is determined more by considerable socioeconomic push and pull factors than by migration policies. The lack of safe, regular, accessible and affordable mobility channels is a major driver for undocumented migration. In fact, when regular migration channels fail to properly reflect labour market needs, especially for low-wage labour, migrants are more likely to be offered undocumented migration solutions by smuggling rings, unethical recruiters and abusive employers:[8] as in other fields of social control, putting a barrier between push and pull factors – without responding to the conditions creating such factors – generally creates underground markets. The term 'illegalization of migrants' draws attention to the factors that contribute to the migrants' 'illegality'.[9]

As well, while globalization has enhanced the relocation of production to developing countries where labour is cheap and workers' protection standards low, if not inexistent, such relocation is not possible for large sectors of the economy, such as agriculture, construction, hospitality, care giving, domestic work, fisheries or extraction, as well as informal work (such as street vendors). In consequence, temporary low-wage workers and undocumented migrants form a pliable workforce for these sectors of the economy, which would not be profitable in an open and regulated labour market in which citizens would request much higher wages for the same tasks. Industrialized countries have therefore created, on their own territory, production conditions similar to those in developing countries, with a view to subsidizing these sectors through the reduction in labour costs.[10] Labour migration is taking place in a context of deregulation of work and labour markets. Salient characteristics of changes in work include precarization of employment, increased informalization of work and economic activity, as well as deteriorating work conditions. Competitive pressures provide an incentive for seeking and hiring labour compelled to accept lowered labour standards, more precarious statuses and 'flexible' employment conditions, in both the Global North and the Global South.[11]

Against this background, *migrants are at heightened risk of exploitation and abuse in the workplace.* Various factors are at play in this process, including:

- deceptive recruitment practices, both by employers and by intermediaries;
- frequent lack of social support systems, including the family networks;
- unfamiliarity with the local culture, language, their rights at work and national labour and migration laws in the country of employment;
- limited or denied access to legal and administrative protection systems, in particular access to unionization, complaint mechanisms, legal representation or the judiciary;

- the generalized absence of effective implementation of labour and occupational health and safety standards through effective labour inspection mechanisms;
- dependence on the job and employer due to migration-related debt, legal status or employers restricting their freedom to leave the workplace;
- reliance by family members on remittances sent back home by the migrant; and
- the general fear of 'sticking their neck out' and jeopardizing the whole personal and family migration project, through protesting, contesting, unionizing or going to court, at the risk of detection, detention and deportation.

These factors are amplified by the discrimination and xenophobia that migrants are increasingly facing everywhere, as well as by the constant pressure to lower the cost of labour in highly competitive sectors.[12]

Migrants routinely work long hours, including overtime for which they are often not paid, and sometimes do not get their breaks or leave entitlements. They frequently report having been misinformed about labour conditions and benefits, and left without access to medical care and consular protection.[13]

Legal status is a factor of economic vulnerability. Temporary migrant workers, migrant domestic workers and migrants in an undocumented situation are the workers most vulnerable to labour exploitation.

Many *temporary migrant workers* are denied the free choice of employment, their work permit and residence authorization being linked to a labour contract with a single employer: they are entirely dependent on this employer not dismissing them, hence vulnerable to abuse. Debt, usually due to recruitment loans taken out with a very high interest rate, is sometimes used to coerce migrants to accept work to which they did not originally agree. Some employers who have paid recruitment fees frequently see the migrants working for them as an economic investment, and therefore try to prevent them from leaving, *inter alia* by confiscating their passports. The confiscation of passports is routinely used as a tool to trap migrants in exploitative jobs, forcing them to perform work they would not agree to otherwise. Temporary migrant workers experience unfair wages, including unequal pay for the same work or work of equal value, based on discriminatory criteria such as nationality. And they have little recourse when wages go unpaid or are paid only after several months.

They usually do not have access to welfare benefits available to long-term residents and may be excluded from wage protection and social security programmes, including health insurance and employment injury coverage. They often live in substandard housing or makeshift accommodation. States generally restrict the rights of temporary migrant workers to family reunification and vocational training. As many spend a short time in a specific area, they may find access to legal services and the judicial system difficult, *inter alia* due to lack of knowledge of the local law, language barriers, cultural isolation and their precarious migration status, as well as restricted right to organize.

Farm work, which is frequently seasonal and performed by temporary or circular migrant workers, is in some countries excluded from labour laws. This makes it very difficult for migrant farm workers to enforce their rights or improve their working conditions. The lack of knowledge of the local language and legislation, including in relation to their labour rights and how to report violations of those rights, means that migrants too frequently do not have access to an effective remedy. Furthermore, fear of retaliation, isolation and lack of resources form considerable barriers in terms of access to protection mechanisms.

Migrant domestic workers constitute another group with a very precarious legal status, starting often with the exclusion of domestic work from the protection of labour or health and safety legislation. They experience 'dependence on the job and employer because of migration-related debt, legal status, practices of employers restricting their freedom to leave the workplace, the simple fact that the migrants' workplace may also be their only shelter'.[14] Poor working and living conditions, including excessive working hours, sometimes without meal or rest breaks, no weekly days off, not being given sufficient food, not being paid for several months and having their passports confiscated, as well as severe physical, psychological and sexual abuse are among the issues often reported by migrant domestic workers. They also suffer threats and intimidation, including threats that their employer will not renew their visa, have them deported, make false allegations to the police about them stealing from the household or throw them out into the streets. Live-in domestic workers are particularly vulnerable to abuse as their workplaces are in private households, behind closed doors and out of the public eye. They are thus physically isolated, which makes it difficult for them to take collective action. The frequent abuse against migrant domestic workers is further aggravated by the lack of labour inspections in private households.[15]

These risks and vulnerabilities are further aggravated for *undocumented migrant workers*, as they often risk deportation if they contact State authorities to seek protection from an abusive employer or if they seek to improve their working conditions through complaining, protesting or publicly mobilizing. Undocumented migrant workers are frequently paid less than the minimum wage, and often experience irregularities with regard to pay such as non-payment or excessive delays in the payment of wages. They often receive their salaries in cash, which makes it difficult to prove when they have not been paid, or when unjustified deductions have been made from their salaries. Some live in abhorrent conditions, in overcrowded houses, without proper sanitation. While undocumented migrant workers are often not able to participate in contributory schemes, they still contribute to financing social protection schemes by paying all indirect taxes. However, social security, including compensation for work accidents, is particularly difficult to access for undocumented migrants.

The fragile status of temporary or undocumented migrant workers results in excessive human and economic costs.

The aforementioned developments result in egregious violations of the human rights and labour rights of migrant workers, as they regularly face discrimination and exploitation in the workplace and sometimes experience forced labour. Migrants often find themselves in debt bondage as a result of exorbitant recruitment fees. A large part of the labour exploitation that they suffer is linked to recruitment agencies which are most often ill-regulated by States. Working through loose chains of sub-agents over several international borders – which makes accountability difficult to implement – some of these agencies extort high recruitment fees and deceive prospective migrants on their prospective salaries, job descriptions, working hours, overtime, days off, lodging and social protection.[16] As previously stated, migrant workers do not have effective recourse and remedies. Perpetrators of abuse, exploitation, violations of rights and violence against migrants too often benefit from practical immunity.

As well, migrant workers often experience de-skilling. The lack of efforts to match job skills to labour demand between countries comes at a cost. It notably increases the proportion of migrant workers who are not working at the skill level that is most relevant to their education, training and work experience. De-skilling hampers both migrant workers' integration into the local labour force and their reintegration into the labour market in the country of origin. The high transaction costs of migrant remittances are another barrier impeding the financial inclusion of migrants.

The growth of informal labour markets has huge political and economic costs for the State. It is difficult to reduce those markets significantly owing to the favourable economic impact of lower labour costs on competitiveness in certain economic sectors, the passive acquiescence of consumers and the indifference of politicians to the wellbeing of persons who live in the shadows, rarely complain and do not vote. States generally invest very few resources in trying to reduce the informal sector. Effective sanctions against abusive employers is most often lacking, despite the fact that it would contribute greatly to reducing the pull factor of undocumented migration, through reducing the attractiveness of undocumented employment, thus reducing the size of the underground labour markets and diminishing the power of exploitative smugglers, recruiters and employers over migrants.[17]

Instead, States prefer criminalizing undocumented entry and stay and strengthening immigration controls. This has led in some countries to cooperation between labour inspection and immigration enforcement and/or imposition of immigration control duties on labour inspectors, employers, landlords or banks. The result impedes effective protection of all migrants under labour law, and also deters migrants from denouncing abusive working conditions and cooperating with labour authorities. The lack of 'firewalls' between public services and immigration enforcement has a huge deterrence effect which keeps undocumented migrants in the 'shadows' and has a disproportionately harmful effect on women, especially in the contexts of domestic violence and sexual assault, and children, especially their access to health care and education.

All migrants, without discrimination, are protected by international human rights law. States have the power to refuse to allow undocumented migrants access to their labour market. But as long as such migrants are in fact working, they are entitled to equal conditions of work, based on the principle of equality and non-discrimination. However, unlike the case of international trade, where the World Trade Organization (WTO) offers a multilateral forum for negotiations on facilitating international trade, no comparable institution exists for negotiations on the facilitation of human mobility.

Migrant workers do not benefit from a clear institutional and practical framework governing the respect, protection and fulfilment of their human rights. Substantive and procedural standards, procedures and institutions, within national and international human rights systems, need to be further developed in order to reinforce migrant workers' status as human beings who are holders of rights, and not simply as productive economic agents or targets of States' sovereign power.

Notes

1 GCIM (Global Commission on International Migration), *Migration in an interconnected world: new directions for action*, November 2005.

2 Koser, K., 'Introduction: international migration and global governance', *Global Governance*, 16, 3 (2010): 301–315; Brickner, R. K., 'Exploring the dynamic intersections of migration, globalization, and the state', in R. K. Brickner (ed.), *Migration, globalization, and the state* (New York: Palgrave Macmillan, 2012), pp. 1–19.

3 Anderson, K. and L. A. Winters, *The challenge of reducing international trade and migration barriers*, Policy Research Working Paper 4598, The World Bank Development Research Group Trade Team, April 2008.
4 UNGA (UN General Assembly), *Report of the Special Rapporteur on the human rights of migrants, François Crépeau*, 'Labour exploitation of migrants', A/HRC/26/35, 3 April 2014; Beatson, J. and J. Hanley, *The exploitation of foreign workers in our own backyards. An examination of labour exploitation and labour trafficking in Canada.* Montreal, Committee of Action Against Human Trafficking National and International, 2015.
5 Marsden, S., 'The new precariousness: temporary migrants and the law in Canada', *Canadian Journal of Law and Society*, 27, 2 (2012): 209–222; Crépeau, F. and I. Atak, 'Global migration governance: avoiding commitments on human rights, yet tracing a course for cooperation', *Netherlands Quarterly of Human Rights*, 34, 2 (2016): 113–146.
6 Cholewinski, R. and P. Taran, 'Migration, governance and human rights: contemporary dilemmas in the era of globalization', *Refugee Survey Quarterly*, 28, 4 (2009): 1–33.
7 Portes, A. 'Toward a structural analysis of illegal (undocumented) immigration', *International Migration Review*, 12, 4 (1978): 469–484.
8 Triandafyllidou, A. and M. Ambrosini, 'Irregular immigration control in Italy and Greece: strong fencing and weak gate-keeping serving the labour market', *European Journal of Migration and Law*, 13, 2011: 251–273.
9 Bauder, H., *Why we should use the term illegalized immigrant*, RCIS Research Briefs No. 2013/1, Toronto, 2013; Dauvergne, C., *Making people illegal: what globalization means for migration and law* (New York: Cambridge University Press, 2008); Düvell, F., 'Paths into irregularity: the legal and political construction of irregular migration', *European Journal of Migration & Law*, 13, 3 (2011): 275–295.
10 Crépeau, F. and I. Atak, 'Global migration governance: avoiding commitments on human rights, yet tracing a course for cooperation', *Netherlands Quarterly of Human Rights*, 34, 2 (2016): 113–146; Global Migration Policy Associates, *A contribution to evaluating the Stockholm Programme regarding migration*, 21 January 2014.
11 Cholewinski, R. and P. Taran, 'Migration, governance and human rights: contemporary dilemmas in the era of globalization', *Refugee Survey Quarterly*, 28, 4 (2009): 1–33.
12 UNGA (UN General Assembly), *Report of the Special Rapporteur on the human rights of migrants, François Crépeau*, 'Labour exploitation of migrants', A/HRC/26/35, 3 April 2014, para 18.
13 UNGA (UN General Assembly), *Report of the Special Rapporteur on the human rights of migrants, François Crépeau*, 'Labour exploitation of migrants', A/HRC/26/35, 3 April 2014, para 19.
14 UN Committee on Migrant Workers, *General Comment No. 1 (2011) on migrant domestic workers*, CMW/C/GC/1, 23 February 2011, para 7.
15 UNGA (UN General Assembly), *Report of the Special Rapporteur on the human rights of migrants, François Crépeau*, 'Labour exploitation of migrants', A/HRC/26/35, 3 April 2014, para 52.
16 UNGA (UN General Assembly), *Report of the Special Rapporteur on the human rights of migrants, François Crépeau*, 'Labour exploitation of migrants', A/HRC/26/35, 3 April 2014, para 67.

17 UNGA (UN General Assembly), *Report of the Special Rapporteur on the human rights of migrants, François Crépeau*, 'Labour exploitation of migrants', A/HRC/26/35, 3 April 2014, para 50; UNGA (UN General Assembly), *Report of the Special Rapporteur on the human rights of migrants, François Crépeau*, 'Towards a 2035 agenda for facilitating human mobility', A/HRC/35/25, 28 April 2017; UNGA (UN General Assembly), *Report of the Special Rapporteur on the human rights of migrants, François Crépeau*, 'Human rights of migrants', A/68/283, 7 August 2012.

3 Precarious work and residence

Ryszard Cholewinski[1]

Introduction

Regulation of admission and residence of non-nationals is often viewed as being at the heart of the sovereign prerogative of States, with the result that the costs experienced by low-skilled migrant workers in terms of their precarious work and residence status remains relatively unexplored. International law also defers to this sovereign prerogative and while international labour standards apply to all workers, the priority afforded immigration enforcement in many countries often overrides their full enjoyment by migrant workers. Moreover, global discussions around migration today are still rooted in the costs–benefits paradigm of the migration and development nexus where the focus has been on measuring economically quantifiable costs that are seen as precluding optimal development outcomes from labour migration, such as the cost of remittance transactions and, more recently, the cost of recruitment.

After a brief examination of the position from the perspective of international labour standards and human rights law, the chapter reflects on how the precarious work and residence status of many low-skilled migrant workers could be addressed in light of the global development agenda, adopted in 2015, and the global compact for safe, orderly and regular migration, which UN Member States have committed to adopt in 2018. Where relevant, examples are also provided of developments at the regional and national level.

Precarious work and residence under international law and at the regional level

The specific situation of migrant workers is regulated by three instruments in international law: the ILO Migration for Employment Convention (Revised), 1949 (No. 97), the ILO Migrant Workers (Supplementary

Provisions) Convention, 1975 (No. 143) and the UN International Convention on the Protection of the Rights of All Migrant Workers and Members of Their Families, 1990.[2]

While none of these instruments purports to interfere with the State sovereign prerogative to regulate the admission and residence of migrant workers in their territory, they contain useful guidance that, if implemented at the national level, could go a long way to mitigate the disadvantages low-skilled migrant workers encounter. For example, Convention No. 97 stipulates that migrants for employment and their family members admitted on a permanent basis to a country are not to be returned because the migrant contracts an illness or injury subsequent to entry,[3] while Convention No. 143 mitigates adverse effects arising out of the common practice of tying work to residence permits by stipulating that migrant workers should not fall into irregular status on loss of employment and should benefit from equal treatment with nationals in respect of guarantees of security of employment, the provision of alternative employment, relief work and retraining.[4] Moreover, Convention No. 143 prohibits restrictions on migrant workers' geographic mobility and only permits tying migrant workers to the same employer for a period not exceeding two years or after completion of the first employment contract if this is shorter in duration.[5] Convention No. 143 also does not preclude State parties from regularizing migrant workers in an irregular status.[6] The 1990 UN Convention contains similar provisions to disconnect work from residence permits and on regularization, but more restrictions are possible regarding free access to the labour market.[7]

At the regional level, free movement of workers is a reality in the European Union (EU), where EU Member States have collectively exercised their sovereignty to do away with restrictions on access to employment for the greater economic good, although practical obstacles remain and resistance to the application of the free movement principle in the United Kingdom was seen as a decisive factor in the vote to leave the EU (Brexit) in the June 2016 referendum. EU law and policy towards third-country nationals, however, is quite different and legal distinctions have been introduced favouring the work and residence of high-skilled over low-skilled workers.[8] The provisions in international law cited above, therefore, are generally not mirrored in the EU directives addressing labour migration from third countries, with the exception of the Employer Sanctions Directive, which enables undocumented migrants to recover unpaid wages, including through the assistance of third parties such as trade unions,[9] although no further provision is made for their continued stay in an EU Member State until the legal proceedings have been concluded.

The European Convention on the Legal Status of Migrant Workers (ECLSMW), adopted under the auspices of the Council of Europe,[10] has fallen into neglect since its effective secretariat, the European Committee on Migration (CDMG) tasked with developing European-wide cooperation on migration, was disbanded in 2012. It applies on the basis of reciprocity among the 11 Council of Europe Member States that have ratified it, including four non-EU/European Economic Area (EEA) Member States, namely Albania, Moldova, Turkey and Ukraine, and contains similar provisions on migrant workers' work and residence to those found in the ILO instruments and the UN Convention. It stipulates that as a rule a work permit issued for the first time should not bind the migrant worker to the same locality or same employer for more than one year – the latter part of this provision is therefore more generous than the equivalent clause in ILO Convention No. 143 discussed above. The Convention stipulates further that the renewal of a migrant worker's work permit should "as a general rule be for a period of at least one year, in so far as the current state and development of the employment situation permits",[11] and also aligns the duration of the residence permit to at least the period of the work permit.[12]

These admittedly imperfect but nonetheless useful provisions in the three international instruments on migrant workers and in the ECLSMW are not reflected in many situations at the national level where loss of employment invariably places migrant workers in situations of irregularity. This situation can be exacerbated in some regions – for example, in the Middle East under the *kafala* (sponsorship) system where in some countries a disproportionate amount of power is afforded to the employer over the worker, not just in the context of their employment in terms of its renewal, termination and ability to transfer to another employer but also with regard to exit from the country.[13] There have been positive reforms in the region to alleviate some of the most exploitative aspects of the system and to ensure that the employment relationship is largely regulated by the labour law.[14] A recent interesting example is that of Bahrain, which has introduced a pilot "flexi permit" scheme by which migrant workers whose work permits have been cancelled or not renewed by their employer can apply for a flexible "sponsor-less" two-year renewable work permit, in effect rendering them self-employed. The fees and costs relating to obtaining such a permit, however, are high and could well deter low-skilled and low-wage migrant workers from applying.[15]

The 2030 Agenda for Sustainable Development, decent work and labour migration

The 2030 Agenda for Sustainable Development pledges that "no one shall be left behind" and commits the global community to realize decent work for all.[16] The concept of decent work as understood by the ILO goes beyond merely having a job, but speaks to the need for a job with rights and social protection and where social dialogue underpins the employment relationship.[17] The 2030 Agenda pays particular attention to decent work in Sustainable Development Goal (SDG) 8 and contains a specific reference to migrant workers, in particular women migrants, in SDG target 8.8 concerned with protection of labour rights and promoting safe and secure working environments for all workers and those in precarious employment, thus underscoring that migrant workers, including those in irregular or undocumented status, also have to be encompassed by this universal commitment.

Giving effect to the decent work elements of the 2030 Agenda, along with its related parts and in particular SDG 10 on reducing inequality within and among countries, which contains SDG target 10.7 on facilitating safe, orderly, regular and responsible migration and mobility of people, including through the implementation of planned and well-managed migration policies, also needs to focus on reducing various labour migration costs. In his 2013 report to the General Assembly in preparation for the Second High-Level Dialogue on International Migration and Development, the UN Secretary-General identified some of these costs as follows:

> There are enormous gains to be made by lowering costs related to migration, such as the transfer costs of remittances and fees paid to recruiters, especially by low-skilled migrant workers. In addition, countries can strengthen the benefits of migration by enhancing the portability of social security and other acquired rights, and by promoting the mutual recognition of diplomas, qualifications and skills.[18]

Unfortunately, the wider and less quantifiable costs associated with precarious work and residence status are not presently captured in the indicators agreed to measure the application of SDG targets 8.8 and 10.7 at the global level, although ILO work on developing and refining the methodology of the two indicators agreed under SDG 8.8 holds promise for identifying the costs relating to the absence of or limitations on freedom of association and collective bargaining for migrant workers and fatal and non-fatal occupational injuries suffered in the workplace.[19] In this connection, a recent ILO study conducted under the auspices of the World Bank's Global Knowledge Partnership on Migration and Development (KNOMAD) has estimated that the costs of deficiencies in conditions of work are substantial and represent 27 per cent of total actual wages.[20] The costs relating to absence of social dialogue and restrictions on worker mobility within destination countries also warrant further examination. With regard to the latter, it has been contended that:

> Restrictions on mobility within destination countries may affect wages for migrant workers and hinder labour market competition. The inability of migrant workers to transition to new employers, including without the approval of their previous employers, is a barrier to appropriate jobs-skills matching and economic productivity, as well as to the freedom of migrant workers to move and negotiate wages.[21]

The task of developing the methodology on the indicator to measure "well-managed migration policies" under SDG 10.7 lies within the responsibility of the International Organization for Migration (IOM) and the Population Division of the UN Department of Economic and Social Affairs (DESA) and this is also where the residence status of low-skilled migrant workers and its relation to precarious work could be specifically addressed, including through policies to regularize those migrants in irregular status, although neither is directly captured in the Migration Governance Index established to inform work on this indicator.[22]

The global compact for safe, orderly and regular migration

The New York Declaration for Refugees and Migrants, adopted by the UN General Assembly in September 2016, was triggered by concerns of the international community with the large movements of refugees and migrants that took place in 2015, particularly in the Mediterranean region, and the resulting policy failures to address these movements. UN Member States committed to adopting two global compacts in 2018, one on refugees and the other for safe, orderly and regular migration. Decent work, labour mobility, a range of migration and development issues, and regularization policies, among others, were identified in the Declaration as matters that could be included in the global compact on migration (GCM).[23] All of these items have subsequently been discussed in the six global thematic consultations on the GCM that have taken place between May and October 2017.[24]

While governments continue to emphasize the role of State sovereignty in the sphere of immigration, important areas of tension have been discussed, such as the need to establish and implement firewalls between immigration enforcement and public services, including labour market institutions, so that migrant workers, including those in irregular status, can enjoy their labour rights without fear of detention and deportation. Greater internal labour market mobility for migrant workers in low-skilled, temporary positions to prevent dependency on a single employer and to reduce exploitation and abuse has also been recommended, as well as ways to take migrant workers out of situations of irregularity, including through national regularization programmes, as a means also of recognizing labour market needs for migrants at all skill levels.[25]

Conclusion

It remains to be seen whether the symbiotic bond between the precarious work and residence of low-skilled migrant workers, which lies at the heart of States' concerns with sovereignty, will be loosened in the context of the GCM negotiations that began in early 2018. Indeed, there is often a political and economic rationale for ensuring the status quo. This is evident in many parts of the world where low-skilled migrant workers are first to be targeted in the event of economic downturns or when governments seek to tackle unemployment of their nationals by reducing the numbers of migrant workers in the labour force. This continues to constitute official policy in many parts of the Middle East, exacerbated by persistent low oil prices and popular concerns about the numbers of migrant workers in certain sectors of the economy, but is also evident in parts of Europe, in particular in light of growing anti-migrant sentiment. Any progress to reduce the costs associated with low-skilled migrants' precarious work and residence under the 2030 Agenda or the GCM would need to be supported, however, by existing international human rights and labour standards. While the specific standards that address these issues directly are invariably limited by the State sovereign principle, they offer important, albeit partial, solutions to longstanding concerns. Indeed, the precarious work and residence of low-skilled migrant workers and how to address it demonstrates that any new global commitments agreed under the 2030 Agenda and the GCM need to take account of the international legal commitments already in place and which require renewed attention.

Notes

1 Senior Migration Specialist, ILO Regional Office for Arab States, Beirut. The views in this article are those of the author and do not in any way represent the views of the ILO or its tripartite constituents.
2 For the text of the ILO instruments, see ILO NORMLEX at www.ilo.org/dyn/normlex/en/f?p=NORMLEXPUB:1:0::NO::: and for the text of the 1990 Convention, see www.ohchr.org/EN/ProfessionalInterest/Pages/CMW.aspx.
3 C97, Art. 8(1). Under Art. 8(2), however, State parties have the discretion not to apply this provision for up to five years from the date of admission.
4 C143, Art. 9.
5 C143, Art. 14.
6 C143, Art. 9(4).
7 See respectively ICRMW, Art. 49, Art. 69 and Art. 52.

8 Compare the Council Directive 2009/50/EC of 25 May 2009 on the conditions of entry and residence of third-country nationals for the purposes of highly qualified employment ("Blue Card" Directive), OJ 2009 L 155/17 to Directive 2011/98/EU of the European Parliament and of the Council of 13 December 2011 on a single application procedure for a single permit for third-country nationals to reside and work in the territory of a Member State and on a common set of rights for third-country workers legally residing in a Member State, OJ 2011 L 343/1 and Directive 2014/36/EU of the European Parliament and of the Council of 26 February 2014 on the conditions of entry and stay of third-country nationals for the purpose of employment as seasonal workers, OJ 2014 L 94/375. The latter Directive, however, provides the option for EU Member States to take account of third-country nationals' previous seasonal employment in the country when considering future applications (Art. 16), although there is no provision for affording a more secure residence status as called for by some stakeholders during the Directive's negotiation.

9 Directive 2009/52/EC of the European Parliament and of the Council of 18 June 2009 providing for minimum standards on sanctions and measures against employers of illegally staying third-country nationals, OJ 2009 L168/24, Arts. 6 and 13.

10 European Treaty Series 93.

11 ECLSMW, Art. 8.

12 ECLSMW, Art. 9.

13 ILO, *Employer–migrant worker relationships in the Middle East: Exploring scope for internal labour market mobility and fair migration*, White Paper, ILO Regional Office for Arab States, Beirut, May 2017, pp. 6–8.

14 Ibid., pp. 13–15.

15 See Bahrain Labour Market Regulatory Authority at http://lmra.bh/portal/en/page/show/325; ILO, *Employer–migrant worker relationships in the Middle East*, above note 13, pp. 14–15.

16 UN, General Assembly, 70th Session, *Transforming our world: The 2030 Agenda for Sustainable Development*, A/RES/70/1 (21 October 2015), Preamble and paras. 3, 4, 9, 26, 27, 48 and 72.

17 See www.ilo.org/global/topics/decent-work/lang--en/index.htm and the four strategic objectives of the ILO Decent Work Agenda in the ILO Declaration on Social Justice for a Fair Globalization, International Labour Conference, 97th Session, June 2008.

18 UN, General Assembly, 68th Session, *International migration and development*, Report of the Secretary-General, A/68/190 (25 July 2013), p. 21, para. 113. The reference to costs associated with recruitment, portability of social security and recognition of education, qualifications and skills is also found in the Addis Ababa Action Agenda of the Third International Conference on Financing for Development, which is recognized as being an integral part of the 2030 Agenda. UN, Third International Conference on Financing for Development, Addis Ababa, 13–16 July 2015, *Outcome document of the Third International Conference on Financing for Development: Addis Ababa Action Agenda*, A/CONF.227/L.1 (15 July 2015), para. 111.

19 For the full list of SDG indicators, see UN, Economic and Social Council, Statistical Commission, 48th Session, *Report of the Inter-agency and Expert Group on Sustainable Development Goal Indicators*, E/CN.3/2017/2 (27 January 2017).

20 M. Aleksynska, S. K. Aoul and V. Petrencu, *Deficiencies in conditions of work as a cost to labor migration: Concepts, extent and implications*, KNOMAD Working Paper 28, August 2017: www.knomad.org/publication/deficiencies-conditions-work-cost-labor-migration-concepts-extent-and-implications.

21 R. Cholewinski and M-J. Tayah, *Promoting decent work for migrant workers*, ILO discussion paper, p. 7 (footnote omitted): www.ilo.org/global/topics/labour-migration/publications/WCMS_344703.

22 The Economist Intelligence Unit, *Measuring well-governed migration: The 2016 Migration Governance Index*, 2016: https://publications.iom.int/system/files/pdf/migration_governance_index_2016.pdf.

23 UN, General Assembly, 71st Session, *New York Declaration for Refugees and Migrants*, A/RES/71/1 (3 October 2016), Annex II.

24 See http://refugeesmigrants.un.org/thematic-sessions.

25 See, in particular, the recommendations in the issues briefs for the first thematic consultation on "Human rights of all migrants, social inclusion, cohesion and all forms of discrimination, including racism, xenophobia and intolerance", and the sixth consultation on "Irregular migration and regular pathways, including decent work, labour mobility, recognition of skills and qualifications and other relevant measures", available at http://refugeesmigrants.un.org/human-rights-all-migrants and http://refugeesmigrants.un.org/labour-mobility respectively.

4 Worker-paid recruitment costs[1]

Dilip Ratha and Ganesh Seshan

Introduction

While there is mounting evidence of the benefits of migrating for employment in terms of its welfare-enhancing aspects for migrants and their families, far less is known about the costs incurred by migrant workers seeking work overseas. The costs paid by migrants for jobs that should otherwise be borne by their foreign employers can represent a significant portion of a migrant's foreign earnings – drastically reducing the net gains from moving abroad.

Recruitment costs paid by migrant workers for low-skilled positions abroad are a major drain on migrants' ability to advance their financial goals. If recruitment costs incurred averaged $5,000 and they were reduced to $1,000 per migrant worker, the cost savings would be $4 billion for every 1 million workers. Reducing such costs would place billions of dollars back into the pockets of poor migrant workers and their families, and could also enhance the efficiency and mutual benefits that can be reaped from labour migration regimes.

In 2015, the Sustainable Development Goals (SDGs) included two migration-related targets: to facilitate orderly, safe, regular and responsible migration (Goal 10.7) and to reduce remittance costs to less than 3 per cent by 2030 and eliminate corridors higher than 5 per cent (Goal 10.c). A World Bank initiative to track remittance costs globally in over 365 corridors has contributed to a momentum in reducing remittance fees, which has dropped from over 10 per cent for sending US$200 in 2011 to 7.2 per cent by the third quarter of 2017.[2] By placing a similar spot-light on recruitment costs, the development community will be in a stronger position to systematically lower costs for the benefit of migrant households and host communities.[3]

This chapter presents several key findings using the KNOMAD-ILO Migration Cost Surveys (MCS) dataset collected as part of an initiative by the Global Knowledge Partnership on Migration and Development (KNOMAD) in partnership with the International Labour Organization (ILO) to develop a methodology on measuring recruitment costs incurred by migrant workers. A primary aim of this project is to work with other United Nation (UN) agencies and national statistical agencies to develop a new SDG indicator 10.7.1, of which the World Bank and ILO are joint custodians. The proposed recruitment cost indicator (RCI) is the average worker-incurred recruitment cost paid for securing an overseas job, expressed as a multiple of monthly foreign earnings.

The chapter is organized as follows: the next section describes the data and key findings and is followed by a discussion of the behaviour of recruitment costs with some recommendations to help reduce it. We conclude in the final section.

Data and findings

Worker-paid recruitment costs can be defined as all the monetary costs incurred by workers (above and beyond those incurred by employers) to establish an employment relationship. Such costs broadly encompass placement fees paid to recruitment agency or to their agents, documentation fees (such as to cover a passport, visa, medical certificate, security clearance or language test), transportation costs and informal payments.[4] While numerous countries legally restrict the amount that workers should pay, poor enforcement oftentimes results in excessive up-front payments.

Until recently, there was no systematic effort to document worker-paid recruitment costs. A joint initiative involving KNOMAD and the ILO undertook purposeful surveys using a standardized questionnaire for interviews with migrant workers between 2014 and early 2017. The data collection and resulting KNOMAD-ILO Migration Cost Surveys (MCS) dataset resulted in new detailed evidence on costs paid in more than 30 bilateral corridors. Surveys were conducted with migrants at various performance sites: in the destination country or in the origin countries at their residence or at the airport – both on arrival from abroad or prior to their departure for jobs overseas.[5] Lacking an appropriate sampling frame, random representative sampling was nearly impossible to conduct, so a snow-ball sampling strategy was used. This approach is likely to have skewed the sample and data reported here as the most vulnerable migrants may not have responded, and as such the costs described should be treated as a lower bound of actual recruitment costs in terms of monthly earnings.

The survey data reveal the following messages: (1) Recruitment costs can be exorbitant, greatly reducing the benefits accruing to migrants and their families. In the case of Pakistani workers in Saudi Arabia, for example, worker-paid recruitment costs varied widely, exceeding in some cases more than 20 months (and at times, 30 months) of earnings (Figure 4.1). (2) The scatter plot also reveals the highly regressive nature of recruitment costs, as these costs were proportionally higher for workers with lower earnings. (3) There is considerable heterogeneity in paid recruitment costs across migration corridors, which can be attributed to both origin and destination country regulatory practices and policies. Also, there are gender-specific differences that likely arise from migration policies targeting specific occupations. (4) In particular, destination country admission policies that regulate the inflow of workers have a noticeable impact on costs. (5) Finally, though more than half of the workers borrowed money to pay for the recruitment expenses, only a small fraction incurred interest payments. We elaborate on these findings in the following paragraphs.

The Pakistan to Saudi Arabia corridor remains one of the costliest in terms of up-front recruitment costs. Costs of over $5,000 or the equivalent of 12 months of a worker's foreign earnings can be observed in the fourth quintile of the distribution (see Figure 4.2).[6] Saudi Arabia was, until the recent workforce nationalization policy (*Nitaqat*), the primary destination for Pakistani migrants, followed by the United Arab Emirates (UAE). Pakistani migrants paid less to move to the UAE, though still far more than other migration corridors. In contrast, workers from the Philippines to Saudi Arabia and Qatar incurred some of the lowest fees, averaging below

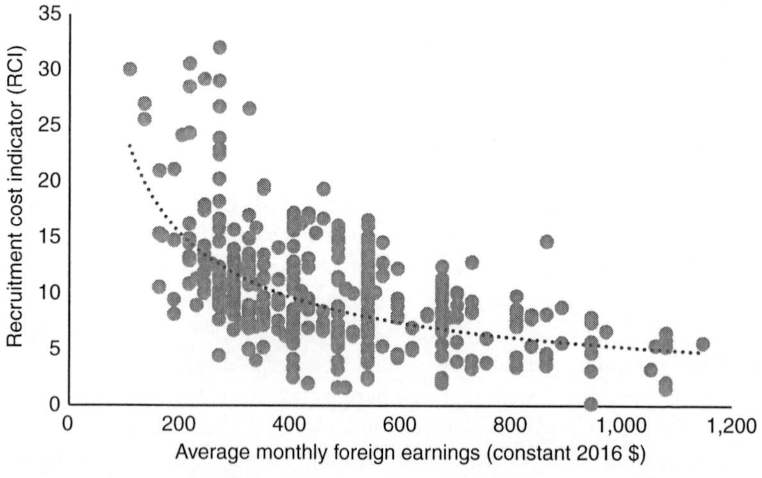

Figure 4.1 Worker-paid recruitment costs for Pakistani workers in Saudi Arabia.
Source: authors' calculation from KNOMAD-ILO MCS dataset.

1.5 times their monthly overseas income. Figure 4.2 also reveals a mostly positive relationship between total recruitment cost and the proposed RCI, implying that high recruitment costs are not offset by larger wages.

In a subset of corridors where migrants of both genders were interviewed, we observe that recruitment costs paid by women are typically lower than those of their male compatriots. The role of gender is particularly pronounced for Filipino migrants (Figure 4.3), and may be indicative of Philippines' policy, which exempts placement fees for those migrants who are hired to work abroad as domestic workers, caregivers and seafarers. However, the enforcement of the no-fee policy seems to vary across corridors – for example, $5 in the Philippines–Saudi Arabia corridor vs $100 in the Philippines–Qatar corridor. Anecdotally, recruitment agents at times circumvent the no-fee policy by imposing additional charges for training.

Recruitment cost also may vary annually due to policies in destination countries that regulate the inflow of foreign workers by country of origin. The Gulf Cooperation Council (GCC) countries are believed to implement country-specific quotas for low-skilled workers, though these are not explicitly published or stated. Figure 4.4 demonstrates the recruitment cost by year of arrival in the case of the Pakistan–Saudi Arabia corridor. Total

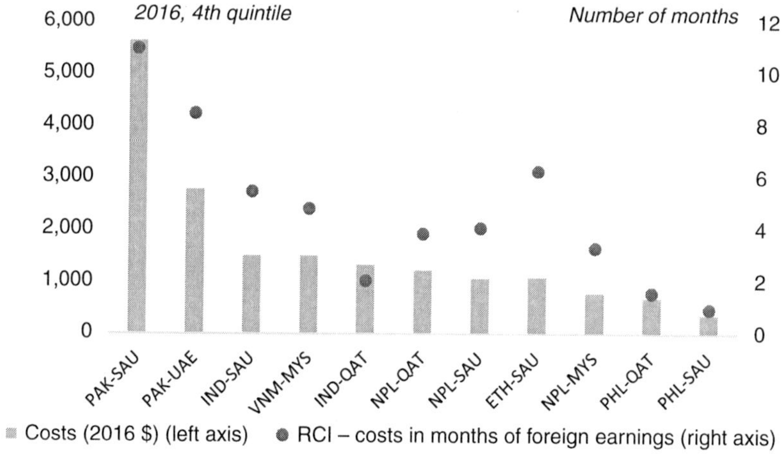

Figure 4.2 Worker-paid recruitment costs by origin–destination corridors.

Source: authors' calculation from KNOMAD-ILO MCS dataset.

Note
ETH = Ethiopia; IND = India; MYS = Malaysia; NPL = Nepal; PAK = Pakistan; PHL = the Philippines; QAT = Qatar; SAU = Saudi Arabia; UAE = United Arab Emirates; VNM = Vietnam.

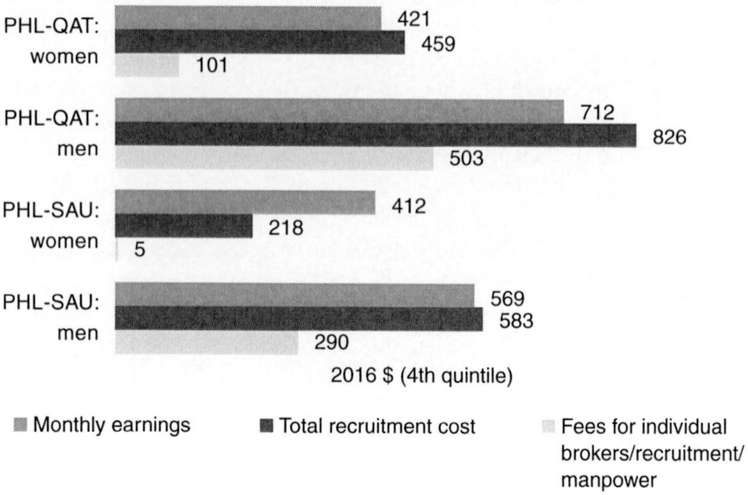

Figure 4.3 Recruitment costs paid by male and female Filipino migrants.

Source: authors' calculation from KNOMAD-ILO MCS dataset.

Note

PHL = the Philippines; QAT = Qatar; SAU = Saudi Arabia.

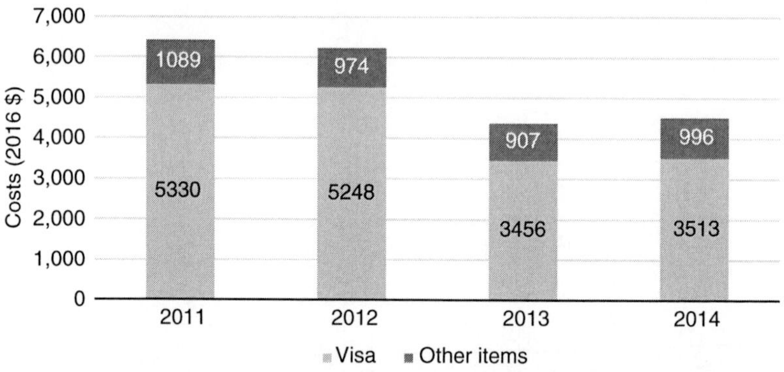

Figure 4.4 Annual variation in costs paid by Pakistani workers to Saudi Arabia.

Source: authors' calculation from KNOMAD-ILO MCS dataset.

costs decreased from 2011 to 2014, and the difference is largely explained by the fall in visa-related charges, which makes up for more than 80 per cent of overall costs incurred.

While formal visa fees are fixed by the receiving country, there is a widespread practice of "visa trading" or "free visas": visas are sold in the black market for sponsored jobs in the GCC that do not exist but provide a means for a worker to "freely" pursue jobs without being bound to a particular employer. The behaviour of visa costs observed in Figure 4.4 appears in line with a destination country admission-policy hypothesis. Consider a (black) market for visas, where quantity of visas demanded decreases with its price and the supply of visas is fixed, based on a predetermined quota set for a country of origin in a given year. When the quota is lowered, thereby reducing the quantity of visas supplied, the market-clearing fees charged by recruiters increase, and vice versa.

In Figure 4.5, we provide additional support for the hypothesis as we document a negative relationship between the total recruitment cost and quota levels proxied by emigration flows in a previous year for three corridors of interest (Pakistan–Saudi Arabia, Pakistan–UAE and Nepal–Qatar).

The ability to raise sufficient funds to meet the up front recruitment costs is critical to a prospective migrant worker's ability to exploit job

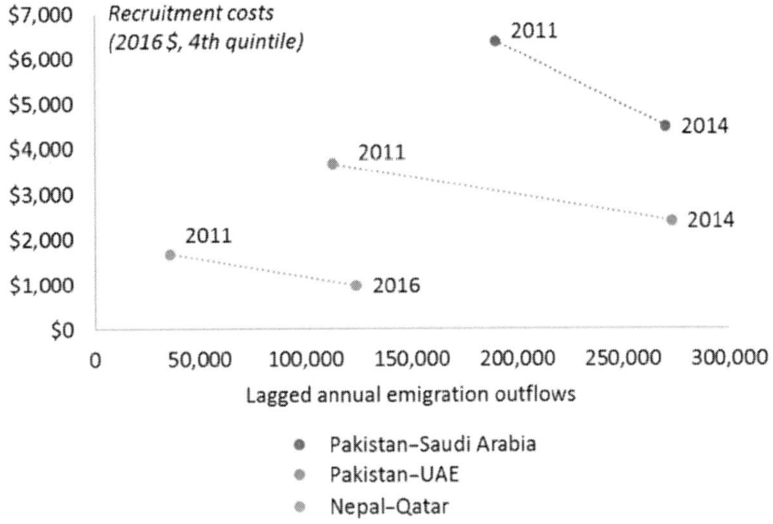

Figure 4.5 Recruitment costs and immigration quotas (proxied by emigration outflows).

Source: authors' calculation from KNOMAD-ILO MCS dataset.

opportunities abroad. As a whole, the data reveal that more than half of the workers borrowed money to pay for the recruitment expenses (see Figure 4.6). On average, the obtained loans covered at least half of the total recruitment costs. Migrants took advantage of both formal and informal lenders – member of household, relatives, friends and money lenders were among the most frequently stated resources.

With the exception of Nepal, less than 30 per cent of migrants reported paying a positive interest rate. Figure 4.6 reports percentage of migrants who took (1) any kind of a loan (the entire bar), (2) loans with no interest incurred (the lower segment of each bar) and (3) loans with positive interest rate (the top portion of each bar). Loans obtained at zero cost were primarily obtained from family and relatives or friends.

In Figure 4.7, we can also observe variation in the interest rates charged at origin, and loan cost based on the subset of migrants who incurred positive loan costs. Given the prevalence of loans, the extent of interest rates charged by lenders can significantly affect the magnitude of recruitment costs. In the case of Pakistanis moving to Saudi Arabia, annual loan charges are equal to 18 per cent of total recruitment costs (excluding loan costs). In contrast, annual loan costs of Nepalese migrants to Malaysia represent less than 3 per cent of their recruitment costs.

While over 60 per cent of Nepalese migrants borrowed at an annualized interest rate of 3 per cent, the minority of Filipinos who paid interest are

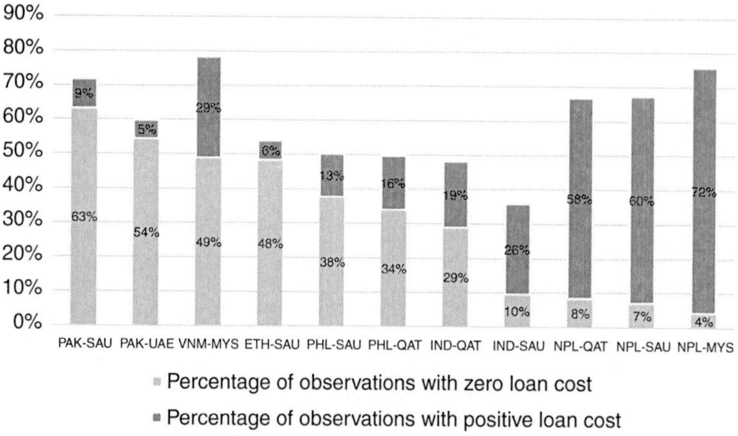

Figure 4.6 Share of migrants with zero and positive loan expenses.

Source: authors' calculation from KNOMAD-ILO MCS dataset.

Note

ETH = Ethiopia; IND = India; MYS = Malaysia; NPL = Nepal; PAK = Pakistan; PHL = the Philippines; QAT = Qatar; SAU = Saudi Arabia; UAE = United Arab Emirates; VNM = Vietnam.

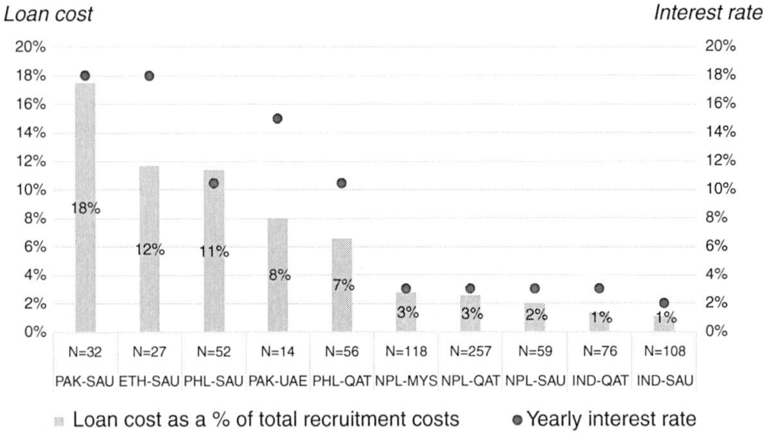

Figure 4.7 Loan costs (percentage of recruitment costs) and interest rate charged.

Source: authors' calculation from KNOMAD-ILO MCS dataset.

Note

ETH = Ethiopia; IND = India; MYS = Malaysia; NPL = Nepal; PAK = Pakistan; PHL = the Philippines; QAT = Qatar; SAU = Saudi Arabia; UAE = United Arab Emirates; VNM = Vietnam.

charged 10 per cent of their loan amount. The inverse relationship between the frequency of positive loan costs and the interest rate offers an alternative explanation to the pattern of zero-cost loans – in countries of origin with expensive loan providers, migrants may resort to borrowing (informally) from family and relatives to avoid high loan charges.

Discussion

Why are recruitment costs so high? The driving forces are the lack of equivalent opportunities at home and increasing restrictiveness of immigration policies. The difficulties of navigating complex migration processes have created a market for brokers or recruitment agencies that are able to circumvent regulations that appear at least on paper to limit costs paid by workers. The illegal practice of "visa trading" in some corridors and excess demand for foreign jobs tend to coalesce into an exploitative setting.

While there is some evidence that bilateral labour agreements (BLAs) between the governments of origin and destination countries help to substantially reduce up-front costs paid at least for the relatively small number of workers that have participated in the various programmes, the scale is minor in comparison to the large number of workers that seek to move abroad to work. Regulatory efforts in origin countries to limit fees have, for the most part, been unsuccessful. The Philippines is gradually moving in favour of exempting any payment of recruitment fees by its migrant workers in all sectors. A zero-fee policy would curtail attempts by recruitment agencies to impose additional charges even when fees are notionally regulated. This would also be consistent with the ILO's Fair Recruitment initiative call for no recruitment fees or related charges to be incurred by workers.

Conclusion

This chapter offers new insights on the magnitude and behaviour of recruitment costs incurred by migrant workers seeking low-skilled positions abroad. Recent data collected as part of a joint initiative by the Global Knowledge Partnership on Migration and Development (KNOMAD) and the International Labour Organization (ILO) to develop a new SDG indicator to monitor recruitment costs reveal substantial corridor-level variation in up-front costs incurred by migrant workers that further vary by gender and across time and are sensitive to policies in both origin and destination countries.

Efforts to reduce recruitment costs would require curbing the exploitative practices and abuses by illegal recruitment agents (or sub-agents), allowing direct recruitment by certified bona fide overseas employers; and bilateral coordination between labour sending and destination countries to ensure greater pathways for regular migration at substantially lower costs.

Notes

1 Excellent research assistance was provided by Petra Niedermayerova.
2 Launched in September 2008, the Remittance Prices Worldwide (RPW) is hosted by the World Bank and monitors remittance prices across all geographical regions of the world.
3 See also Abella, M. and Martin, P. (2014). *Migration costs of low-skilled labor migrants: Key findings from Pilot Surveys in Korea, Kuwait and Spain*. Global Knowledge Partnership on Migration and Development (KNOMAD) Technical Report; Abella, M. and Martin, P. (2016). *Worker-paid migration costs: Key findings from 2015 surveys in Pakistan, Ethiopia and Nepal*. Global Knowledge Partnership on Migration and Development (KNOMAD) Technical Report; Global Forum on Migration and Development. (2016). "GFMD RT 1.1 Reducing migration costs". Background Paper, 10 November 2016; International Labour Organization. (2015). *Bilateral agreements and memoranda of understanding on migration of low skilled workers: A review*. Geneva; International

Labour Organization. (2016). *General principles and operational guidelines for fair recruitment*. Geneva; International Labour Organization. (2016). *The cost of migration: What low-skilled migrant workers from Pakistan pay to work in Saudi Arabia and the United Arab Emirates*. Islamabad; Stark, O. and Bloom, D. E. (1985). "The new economics of labor migration". *The American Economic Review*, 75(2), 173–178; World Bank. (2017). *Migration and development brief 28*, 27 October; World Bank. (2017). *Remittances prices worldwide*. Issue 23, September 2017; World Bank. (2017). "KNOMAD-ILO Migration costs surveys". Global Knowledge Partnership on Migration and Development (KNOMAD).

4 At present, the cost of servicing migration loans is currently excluded.

5 Lessons learnt from these experiences are being used to produce guidelines to support national statistical agencies in collecting costs data on a regular basis as part of their SDG monitoring initiatives.

6 The rationale for reporting the fourth quintile is that policy-makers should focus on migrants who are burdened by relatively high recruitment costs. It also mitigates concerns about large outlier values.

5 (In)equality in wages and working conditions

*Bjarney Friðriksdóttir**

Introduction

The principle of equal treatment in wages and working conditions as it is enshrined in international human rights and labour law provides that migrant workers are entitled to enjoy the right to equal treatment with nationals in the state where they work. Migrant workers, particularly those who are considered 'temporary' and/or classified as low-skilled workers, are frequently excluded from equal treatment with nationals in wages and working conditions by law or in practice. This chapter will outline some of the relevant human rights and labour law standards and give examples of discriminatory laws and practices that exclude migrant workers from enjoying equal treatment in wages and/or working conditions, as well as the consequences thereof.

International human rights and labour law standards

The International Covenant on Economic, Social and Cultural Rights (ICESCR), recognizes the 'right of everyone' to among other rights, the right to work, which includes the right to the opportunity to gain a living by work freely chosen or accepted, the enjoyment of just and favourable conditions of work, to form trade unions and join a trade union of own choice and the right to social security, including social insurance.[1] In addressing the personal scope of the Covenant in relation to non-nationals, the UN Committee on Economic, Social and Cultural Rights established that the Covenant 'applies to everyone including non-nationals, such as refugees, asylum-seekers, stateless persons, migrant workers and victims of international trafficking, regardless of legal status and documentation'.[2] Additionally, as regards a person's economic and social situation, the Committee has confirmed that 'individuals and groups of individuals must not be arbitrarily treated on account of belonging to a certain economic or social group or strata within society'.[3] The right to just and favourable conditions of work[4] enshrined in the Covenant addresses, among other factors, the right to fair wages and equal remuneration for work of equal value without distinction of any kind, safe and healthy working conditions and rest, leisure and reasonable limitations of working hours. These rights apply to 'all workers in all settings', including workers in the informal sector, migrant workers, workers from ethnic and other minorities, domestic workers and refugee workers.[5] Whereas migrant workers, in particular if their status is irregular, are vulnerable to exploitation, long working hours, unfair wages and dangerous and unhealthy working environments, states party to the Covenant should guarantee that laws and policies ensure that migrant workers enjoy treatment that is no less favourable than that of national workers in relation to remuneration and conditions of work.[6] The International Convention on the Protection of the Rights of all Migrant Workers and Members of their Families (ICRMW) contains in Article 25, applicable to all migrant workers, analogous standards to those in the ICESCR regarding equal treatment with nationals in wages and working conditions and provides that it shall not be lawful to derogate from the principle of equal treatment with nationals in private contracts of employment.[7]

All international labour law adopted by the International Labour Organization (ILO) applies to migrant workers and there are two ILO Conventions that particularly address migrant workers: Convention No. 97, Migration for Employment, and Convention No. 143, Migrant Workers. The personal scope of Convention No. 97 is limited to migrants regularly admitted for employment. The central provision of it, in terms of protection of the rights of migrants, addresses non-discrimination and provides that states party to it undertake to apply treatment no less favourable than that which it applies to its own nationals in respect to remuneration, including family allowances, hours of work, holidays and pay, minimum age for employment, women's work and the work of young persons, membership of trade unions and enjoyment of the benefits of collective bargaining and accommodation, without discrimination in respect of nationality, race, religion or sex, to immigrants lawfully within its territory.[8] ILO Convention No. 143, Migrant Workers, similarly requires state parties to guarantee equality of treatment, pertaining to working conditions, for all migrant workers who perform the same activity whatever might be the particular conditions of their employment.[9]

In a general assessment on the scope of Conventions No. 97 and No. 143, the ILO Committee of Experts has provided that the 'instruments do not distinguish between workers who migrate for permanent settlement, and those who migrate for short-term or seasonal work and who do not expect to stay for any significant length of time in the host country'. That, other than for certain provisions that apply explicitly only to permanent migrant workers, 'no exemptions are envisaged in relation to any category of regular-entry migrant worker'.[10] Domestic workers, many of whom are migrants, particularly women, have the right to equal treatment with nationals in all aspects related to wages and working conditions. ILO Convention No. 189, concerning decent work for domestic workers, reiterates that both Conventions No. 97 and No. 143 are of special relevance to domestic workers while many of them are migrants, but Convention No. 189 is set forth recognizing the special conditions under which domestic work is carried out that make it desirable to supplement general ILO standards with standards specific to domestic workers so as to enable them to enjoy their rights fully.[11] Convention No. 189 recalls several of the fundamental rights at work and requires state parties to take measures to respect, promote and realize these fundamental principles and rights at work.[12] The Convention stipulates that each state party shall take measures towards ensuring equal treatment between domestic workers and workers generally in relation to normal hours of work, overtime compensation, periods of daily and weekly rest and paid annual leave,[13] and requires each state party to ensure that domestic workers enjoy minimum wage coverage, where such coverage exists, and that remuneration is established without discrimination based on sex.[14] The right of each domestic worker to enjoy a safe and healthy working environment is reiterated and states party to it are required to take effective measures to ensure the occupational safety and health of domestic workers.[15]

Exclusion of low-skilled and 'temporary' workers from equal treatment

Certain categories of migrant workers, mostly classified as low-skilled or temporary workers, are reported to be excluded from the scope of protection of national labour or employment laws, including provisions on equality and non-discrimination. Among these groups of workers that are excluded[16] by some member states of the ILO are workers in agriculture,[17] including in particular workers on family farms and other small agricultural undertakings,[18] casual or temporary workers[19] and domestic workers.[20]

By conducting a survey along seven migration corridors linking selected Gulf, Asian and African countries that are particularly known for the intensity of labour migration, the KNOMAD project has collected data on low-skilled labour migrants which provide measures of losses incurred by migrants due to deficiencies in the conditions of work abroad. Analysis of the data reveals that:

> nearly 14.7 percent did not receive wages on time, and, when remunerated, 23.1 percent reported they received wages that were lower than those promised before the departure. Over half of the migrant workers reported hours of work that were greater than the authorized total hours of work, including overtime, as per national and international standards. The average number of reported hours per week is 71, and a quarter of the migrants reported systematically not having any rest day per week.[21]

Additionally, one-third of the migrants experienced health-related problems, 'of which about 15 percent had serious work-related injuries, which is far above national averages'. Two immigrants in five were not paid for days lost due to health problems and over half of the migrant workers reported not having the same wage as the native-born workers.[22]

The survey collected information on additional factors to those addressed above and when all these factors were taken together in an attempt to calculate aggregated monetary losses to low-skilled migrants due to deficiencies in conditions of work abroad, the loss was found to 'represent at least 30 percent of total promised wages or 27 percent of total actual wages', and those costs are estimated to be 'twice as high as the recruitment and travel costs incurred to effectuate the migration'.[23] The three sets of measures used in the survey focused on *total wage loss due to wage shortfall, total wage loss due to hours problems* and *total wage loss due to health and social security problems.* When taken together to obtain a summary measure of *aggregate losses due to deficiencies in conditions of work abroad*, the findings of the project show that these aggregate losses are positive for 89.3 per cent of the migrants in the sample, that even 'for those who reported no losses due to misinformation in terms of actual salary, 86 percent of the migrants had positive losses due to excessive hours or unremunerated injuries and sickness'.[24] The findings of the project further reveal that the costs associated with the conditions of work 'vary with individual characteristics, especially age, gender, occupations and skills', and that the aggregate losses due to poor conditions of work are substantially higher for women than for men. Female domestic workers 'have some of the highest costs associated with deficiencies in labor conditions, and especially with prohibitively excessive hours'.[25]

In European Union law, posted workers are excluded from enjoying equal treatment with nationals in wages and working conditions in the state where they work as they are not considered to be a part of the EU labour market, although they may work in member states of the EU for an unlimited amount of time. Posted workers hold employment contracts with undertakings that are based in a state other than the state in which they perform their work and the contracts are governed by the law of the state where the enterprise is based and not the state where they perform their work. Article 3 of the posted workers directive, on terms and conditions of employment, addresses among other factors minimum work periods and maximum rest periods, paid annual holidays, health, safety and hygiene at work and wages. As regards wages, it provides that posted workers should be guaranteed minimum rates of pay, including overtime rate, as defined by the national law and/or practice of the state to whose territory the worker is posted.[26]

In a problem analysis of the directive, the reference to minimum level of pay is considered to create an un-level playing field for companies due to different rules on wages between posted and local workers, which results in social dumping and unfair competition.[27] Posted workers are reported to receive a lower remuneration level than local workers, especially in high-wage EU receiving countries, such as Belgium, Denmark, France, Germany, the Netherlands and Sweden. Because of the absence of data on the earnings of posted workers, only gross estimates exist. However, the wage gap (in compliance with the directive) is estimated to range from 10 to 15 per cent in the Danish construction sector, up to about 25–35 per cent in the construction sector in the Netherlands and Belgium, and up to 50 per cent in the road transport sector in Belgium.[28] According to the latest data available, from 2014, there were over 1.92 million postings in the EU,[29] which constitutes 0.7 per cent of the total EU workforce. Postings are concentrated in a few sectors of the economy: 42 per cent of total postings are concentrated in construction, 21.8 per cent in the manufacturing industry, 13.5 per cent in other service sectors, such as personal services (education, health and social work) and 10.3 per cent in business services (administrative, professional and financial services).[30]

Conclusions

The right to equal treatment of migrant workers with nationals in wages and working conditions is a fundamental human right related to work. International human rights and labour law does not permit derogations from this principle based on differences in length of contract or the type of work the migrant is engaged in. Excluding selected groups of migrant workers from enjoying the right to equal treatment with nationals, in law and/or in practice, contravenes international standards. The case of posted workers in the European Union shows that requiring only minimum standards, rather than equality, results in the earnings of posted workers being 10–50 per cent lower than those of national workers in the sectors where most posted workers are concentrated. The findings of the KNOMAD project reveal substantial costs to low-skilled migrant workers due to wages paid being lower than provided for by employment contracts, excessive working hours and lack of protection in cases of health problems and injuries sustained at work. Additionally, over half of the migrant workers that participated in the survey reported being subjected to discrimination based on nationality in regard to wages. Systematic discrimination against migrant workers, in law and/or practice, enables exploitation of these workers and denying them equal treatment with nationals constitutes social dumping and contravenes international human rights and international labour law standards.

Notes

* The views in this article are those of the author and do not in any way represent the views of the OHCHR.

1 Article 6 ICESCR.

2 Committee on Economic, Social and Cultural Rights, General Comment No. 18, The right to work (Art. 6), (2005), para 30.

3 Committee on Economic, Social and Cultural Rights, General Comment No. 20, Non-discrimination in economic, social and cultural rights (2009), para 35.

4 Article 7 ICESCR.

5 Committee on Economic, Social and Cultural Rights, General Comment No. 23 on the right to just and favourable conditions of work (Article 7), (2016), para 5.

6 Ibid., para 47(e).

7 Article 25(2) ICRMW.

8 Article 6(1) ILO Convention No. 97.

9 Article 12(g) ILO Convention No. 143.

10 International Labour Conference, 105th Session 2016, *Promoting Fair Migration, Report of the Committee of Experts on the Application of Covenants and Recommendations (articles 19, 22 and 35 of the Constitution), Report III (Part 1 B)*. Geneva: International Labour Office, para 109.

11 ILO Convention No. 189, paras 7 and 8 of preamble.

12 Article 3 ILO Convention No. 189.

13 Article 10 ILO Convention No. 189.

14 Article 11 ILO Convention No. 189.

15 Article 13 ILO Convention No. 189.

16 International Labour Conference, 105th Session 2016, *Promoting Fair Migration, Report of the Committee of Experts on the Application of Covenants and Recommendations (articles 19, 22 and 35 of the Constitution), Report III (Part 1 B)*. Geneva: International Labour Office, para 329.

17 For example, Plurinational State of Bolivia, Jordan and the United States.

18 For example, Saudi Arabia, United Arab Emirates and Yemen.

19 For example, Angola, Qatar, Saint Kitts and Nevis, Sudan, Syrian Arab Republic and Yemen.

20 For example, Egypt, Gambia, Japan, Kuwait, Oman, Qatar, Saudi Arabia, Singapore, Sudan, Syrian Arab Republic, Tuvalu, United Arab Emirates, United States and Yemen.

21 Aleksynska, Mariya, Samia Kazi Aoul, Veronica Petrencu, 2017, 'Deficiencies in Conditions of Work as a Cost to Labor Migration: Concepts, Extent, and Implications', KNOMAD Working Paper No. 28, 44.
22 Ibid.
23 Ibid.
24 Ibid., 38.
25 Ibid., 45.
26 Directive 96/71/EC of 16 December 1996 concerning the posting of workers in the framework of the provision of services, Article 3(1).
27 Commission Staff Working Document, Impact Assessment, Accompanying the document Proposal for a Directive of the European Parliament and the Council amending Directive 96/71/EC concerning the posting of workers in the framework of the provision of services, SWD(2016) 52, 8 March 2016, 10.
28 Ibid., 13.
29 Ibid., 6.
30 Ibid., 8.

6 The health costs of irregular migration

Alyna C. Smith

Introduction

Policy responses to migration give rise to significant health-related vulnerabilities. As globalization pushes millions to seek security and opportunity outside their country or region of origin, many of them do so at their peril, because they have few regular and safe pathways to migrate. The result is that, for many, migrating carries an incalculable health cost. Moreover, for the millions residing outside their country of origin, being undocumented means they are generally shut out from regular job markets, social safety nets, and health systems. They are denied the benefit of a country's laws protecting workers and victims, and are exposed to a heightened risk of exploitation by employers, landlords, spouses, and others, enduring silently because the risk of being detained and deported outweighs the likelihood of getting assistance or justice if they report abuse. The negative impact on mental and physical health of being undocumented is therefore multifaceted and profound.

Fortunately, there is growing recognition in international fora of the need to address migrants' health; the New York Declaration for Refugees and Migrants agreed by world leaders on 19 September 2016[1] contains several references to health; and a statement by Government health ministers in February 2017 affirms their recognition of the right to health of every human being, regardless of status.[2] But current discussions focus almost exclusively on humanitarian responses, or in some cases on the necessity of adapting health systems to respond to diverse populations or to "vulnerability", neglecting, or avoiding, discussion of the underlying reasons that migrants may face disparate health risks and outcomes.

This chapter takes a broader approach to migrant health, looking at the health-related costs of irregular migration, with a focus on the European Union. It examines the impact on migrants' health of policies that affect the conditions in which they migrate and the conditions in which they live once they have migrated, as well as their ability to access health services in the EU. Finally, it considers the cost of these policies on the broader society, and suggests what needs to happen to turn things around.

The right to health for migrants

It is useful to begin with a reminder of states' obligation in the sphere of health towards people, including those living within, or who may have entered, their territory irregularly.

Under international human rights law,[3] states have a duty to ensure the right to health, among other things by taking concrete steps towards realizing universal health care, as well as the preconditions for health. Significantly, these measures must be pursued in a manner that does not discriminate based on residence status.[4] In addition to these positive obligations, states also have a duty to *refrain* from doing certain things that undermine the right to health.[5] The UN committee charged with overseeing states' progress in meeting their obligations in relation to economic and social rights has described several examples of how a state can fail in this duty to respect the right to health:

- "denial of access to health facilities, goods and services to particular individuals or groups";
- "adoption of laws or policies that interfere with the enjoyment of the any of the components of the right to health";
- "failure of the State to take into account its obligations regarding the right to health when entering into bilateral or multilateral agreement with other States, international organizations and other entities".[6]

The scope of a state's duties under the right to health, and thus for state accountability, therefore extend beyond its citizens to everyone within its territory, irrespective of migration status; and beyond policies and practices within the sphere of health to those that *affect* health – including agreements with third countries. As we will see, the EU demonstrates how health is utterly absent from any assessment of the cost of policies addressing migrants in an irregular situation.

The health-related costs of irregular migration and irregular status

The health-related costs of denying access to health services

Health-related vulnerabilities are compounded by the fact that, in the majority of European countries, the right to health is conditioned on the right to reside. In the United Kingdom, which has a national health service (NHS), whether one receives free care depends on one's right to remain indefinitely in the UK. Those without this right have to pay a surcharge to benefit from many non-emergency services, or be charged out of pocket. To determine who is chargeable for care, the NHS can ask the Home Office – and if the patient is in the country irregularly, the Home Office can proceed with immigration enforcement.[7] This has a notable chilling effect on health-seeking behaviour, for a segment of the population already exposed to multiple vulnerabilities.[8]

Germany is one of many European countries with an insurance-based health system, which means that access to coverage is largely based on one's employment situation. Asylum-seekers and undocumented residents can access the health system without insurance by obtaining vouchers (*krankenschein*) from the social welfare office for necessary care. This same office has a duty to inform immigration officials when it becomes aware that a patient is without proper status. Evidently, this reporting duty acts as a major deterrent to making use of health services.[9]

There is overall significant variation across EU member states in the rights granted to non-nationals to freely access national health systems, but the general trend is one of exclusion. People who are without proper residence status have no entitlement to primary and secondary care in the large majority of member states. Five EU member states limit their legal entitlement to emergency care only, and seven member states make no specific provision for maternity care for undocumented women in their laws. Of the ten member states that provide some degree of primary or secondary care, in only eight are those entitlements meaningful, in so far as they include access free of charge.[10] The diversity and complexity of rules regulating undocumented migrants' right to access health care in the EU, as well as the vagueness of some of the language defining their entitlements,[11] has naturally led to confusion not only among migrants themselves, but also among health care professionals, and contributes to the inconsistent application of those rules and mistaken denial of care.[12]

This exclusion from care has a cost for society as well. In September 2015, the EU Fundamental Rights Agency (FRA) published a report[13] on the financial impact on health systems of excluding undocumented migrants from accessing non-emergency care, looking at the examples of hypertension and prenatal care in Germany, Greece, and Sweden. According to the study's findings, which are based on economic modelling, Germany and Greece would, after two years, see savings of up to 48 per cent of health system costs, and Sweden up to 69 per cent, if prenatal care were made equally available to pregnant undocumented women. Significantly, the study does not consider other costs to the health system, or to individuals, their families, or society, of the long-term effect of low birth weight. Nor does it look at the costs of communicable diseases or mental health conditions that go undiagnosed and untreated, for the individual, their family, and health systems, which one can assume would be substantial. A peer-reviewed research article, published in July 2015,[14] similarly concludes that the cost of providing restricted access to health care for asylum-seekers and refugees in Germany is higher than granting them regular access.

Public health goals are also compromised by exclusionary policies. The European Centre for Disease Control (ECDC) gathers data on the HIV infection among migrants, and has reported that HIV disproportionately affects migrants, but that there is "growing evidence that sub-groups are at risk of acquiring HIV after arrival in the EU/EEA".[15] This presents a critical opportunity for prevention; however, nearly half of EU/EEA countries report major gaps in testing services for undocumented migrants, with several reporting "major gaps in testing services for migrants from high-prevalence countries, [men who have sex with men] and sex workers". Meanwhile, just 16 EU countries grant the right to HIV screening, regardless of status – and just 11 of these allow access to treatment.[16]

Health professionals also pay a price for policies and practices that define access to health services based on migration status. In EU member states with an explicit policy of sharing information about patients' migration status between health authorities and immigration authorities, or which do not have rules protecting the privacy and confidentiality of their personal information, health professionals may be seen as complicit with migration enforcement officials.[17] This fundamentally undermines patients' trust in health providers, and in the health care system, and deters them from seeking medical assistance until they reach a point of crisis.[18] Health professionals also feel torn between their ethical obligations to provide non-discriminatory care, and laws that require them to screen patients based on their residence status. And they are also affected by disparate rules about charging and reimbursement that vary based on the status of the patient, and impose burdensome administrative processes that may create incentives to turn people away.[19]

The health-related costs of precarious working conditions

There is also a significant health cost to people living and working with irregular status in Europe. Despite safeguards for undocumented workers under EU law, with few exceptions, undocumented workers in Europe cannot safely report excessively low or unpaid wages, unsafe working conditions, or other forms of ill-treatment. The result is greater exposure to exploitation, poverty, injury, and death, with limited recourse to the justice or health care system.[20] At the same time, people living and working with irregular status often occupy and support entire sectors of the economy,[21] and through remittances contribute massively to social systems in their countries of origin.

The result is insecurity, exposure to exploitation, and inability to claim protection for their basic rights. Studies show higher rates of fatal and non-fatal injuries among migrant workers compared to native populations, in part because they are over-represented in higher risk occupations.[22] These include construction and agriculture, as well as sectors dominated by women, such as the hair, nail, and beauty industry,[23] with its high level of exposure to harsh and often hazardous chemicals;[24] and domestic work, whose informal and atypical nature is associated with social exclusion, confinement and isolation, low pay, long working hours, strenuous and hazardous work – all combined with a lack of health care and social protection.[25]

The health-related costs of Europe's migration policies

In 2015, in response to a spike in the number of irregular migrants arriving at its borders, the European Union adopted a new migration agenda that entrenched the dichotomy between migrants deserving of protection and migrants susceptible to swift return.[26] These policies reinforce the EU's long term aim to "end irregular migration", by stopping people from migrating and returning those in the Union irregularly, with success being defined by the number of new arrivals and the rate of returns. Indeed, one year following implementation of a deal between the EU and Turkey to stop the movement of migrants, its implementation was described by the EU as generating "positive results", a "continued trend of progress", with some member states championing replication of the model with other countries.[27]

What is left out is other measures, namely the human and financial costs of a deterrence-oriented policy. From 1993 to November 2012, 14,600 people are estimated to have perished while attempting to cross the EU's southern border – with the number swelling to over 17,000 when the definition is widened to include deaths attributed to immigration and border policies, such as deaths in detention and while crossing land borders.[28] According to Médecins Sans Frontières, since the implementation of the EU–Turkey deal in March 2016, and the closing of the Balkan routes, "movement of people has never stopped, but their routes are fragmented and their journeys have become increasingly dangerous". They report that more than 140 people have died along the Balkan route, drowned in the Aegean Sea, freezing to death at land borders, or linked to conditions in camps in Greece.[29]

The EU does not keep figures on the number of people in immigration detention. A 2014 study estimated that over 90,000 people were detained in 22 EU countries and Norway.[30] Detention is both a well-known cause of diminished physical and mental health,[31] and a place where access to adequate health care is generally limited.[32] The result is a double blow to the health of people in detention, particularly those with special needs, such as pregnant women, and children,[33] with potential lifelong consequences. Health professionals have spoken out forcefully about the significant harm caused by detention on the health of children,[34] young people, and their families,[35] and noted that many children experience the actual process of being detained as a newly traumatizing experience.[36]

A 2011 study of people with HIV in immigration detention found repeated interruptions and disruptions of antiretroviral (ARV) therapy, the occurrence of demeaning and degrading practices that worsened individuals' conditions, and the deportation of people with HIV with less than a three-month supply of ARVs.[37] Detention also has harmful effects for LGBTI people, whose needs are often overlooked and who may not be immediately or obviously recognized as LGBTI. Detaining LGBTI migrants alongside people who discriminate against them increases the likelihood of detrimental effects on their mental and physical health.

The health-related cost of the EU's migration policy is therefore undeniable and significant, with far-reaching and long-lasting negative effects on migrants' physical health and wellbeing.

What needs to happen

The universal right to health imposes an obligation on states to provide appropriate, accessible, and quality services – to everyone on their territory, not only to their citizens. The chasm between migrants' right to health and states' behaviour, in practice, is in part a result of the fact social systems have not caught up with the realities of globalization. And while states strive to maximize the benefits of migration for their economies, they often do so by viewing migrants as economic units, to whom they ostensibly owe little by way of social rights and protection; or as threats to existing social systems, likely to undermine them through free-riding.

This means that migrants are exposed to enormous health costs – costs in being forced to migrate in extraordinarily risky ways, or to work unprotected in often exploitative settings and high-risk sectors of the economy. And despite their contributions to the economic and social fabric of their countries of residence, they are largely excluded from benefitting from social systems, to the detriment of their health and wellbeing, as well as to the broader community and to the health system itself.

So what needs to change? Discussions about migration – and mobility – must begin to systematically include discussions about social as well as labour rights and protections, and to address the damaging effects of linking social rights to residence status. And there must also be a recognition of how the existing migration apparatus creates enormous health-related risks for the millions of individuals and families.

At the national level, this means giving a voice to those who have stepped into the breach, for reasons of ethics, pragmatism, and humanity,[38] to better understand the human and social consequences of exclusion; and to include migrants themselves and the organizations that champion their rights in the development of policies. The UN global compact on migration represents a critical opportunity to address migration in a way that integrates the perspective of people who migrate for a diversity of reasons, all in response to the call of security and opportunity, to ensure that the health-related costs of irregular migration are recognized and concretely addressed in a manner that is anchored in human rights and dignity.

Notes

1 New York Declaration, available at http://refugeesmigrants.un.org/declaration.
2 "Colombo Statement", issued 23 February 2017 following the High-level meeting of the Global Consultation on Migrant Health, Colombo, Sri Lanka.
3 CESCR General Comment No. 14: The Right to the Highest Attainable Standard of Health (Article 12).
4 Following the adoption of the New York Declaration for Refugees and Migrants in September 2016, the UN Committee on Economic, Social and Cultural Rights issued a strong statement on the duties of states towards migrants: "The Committee has made it clear that protection from discrimination cannot be made conditional upon an individual having a regular status in the host country." It goes further, stating that the inability of migrants to access health care and to avail themselves of other social rights because of their irregular status "cannot be tolerated". Statement by the Committee on Economic, Social and Cultural Rights (13 March 2017), "Duties of States Towards Refugees and Migrants Under the International Covenant on Economic, Social and Cultural Rights".
5 A. E. Yamin (2005), "The Right to Health Under International Law and Its Relevance to the United States", *American Journal of Public Health*, 95(7): 1156–1161. www.ncbi.nlm.nih.gov/pmc/articles/PMC1449334/.
6 CESCR General Comment No. 14: The Right to the Highest Attainable Standard of Health (Article 12), at para. 50.
7 See, e.g., Maternity Action (March 2017), "The Impact on Health Inequalities of Charging Migrant Women for NHS Maternity Care: A Scoping Study".
8 P. Chauvin, C. Vuillermoz, N. Simonnot, F. Vanbiervliet, M. Vicart, A-L. Macherey, and V. Brunel (May 2015), "Access to Healthcare for People Facing Multiple Vulnerabilities in Health in 26 Cities across 11 Countries. Report on the Social and Medical Data Gathered in 2014 in Nine European Countries, Turkey and Canada", Paris: MdM.

9 For EU nationals, the right to social benefits is also conditioned on the right to reside. Increased mobility within Europe has traditionally been grounded in the contributions of the European worker to the host country, and there has been significant resistance to the expansion from a purely "market citizen" to a "European social citizen", entitled to social benefits not tied exclusively to economic activity. See Eva-Maria Poptceva (2014), "Freedom of Movement and Residence of EU Citizens: Access to Social Benefits", *European Parliamentary Research Service*.

10 PICUM (2016), "Sexual and Reproductive Health Rights of Undocumented Migrants: Narrowing the Gap Between Their Rights and the Reality in the EU".

11 For instance, to "care that cannot be deferred" in Sweden; to "essential or urgent care" in Belgium, and "medically necessary care" in the Netherlands; and to "emergency" care only in many countries.

12 See MIPEX Health Strand; Sarah Spencer and Vanessa Hughes (July 2015), "Outside and In: Legal Entitlements to Health Care and Education for Migrants with Irregular Status in Europe", COMPAS, Oxford University; AAIDS Action Europe report on access for undocumented migrants: "Restricted Access to Antiretroviral Treatment for Undocumented Migrants: A Bottle Neck to Control the HIV Epidemic in the EU/EEA".

13 EU Agency for Fundamental Rights (2015), "Cost of Exclusion from Healthcare: The Case of Migrants in an Irregular Situation".

14 Kayvan Bozorgmehr and Oliver Razum (22 July 2015), "Effect of Restricting Access to Health Care on Health Expenditures among Asylum Seekers and Refugees: A Quasi-Experimental Study in Germany, 1994–2013".

15 ECDC (2016), "Country Level Implementation of the Dublin Declaration on HIV/AIDS in the EU and EECA", http://ecdc.europa.eu/en/healthtopics/aids/Documents/hiv%20dublin%20declaration%20special%20report%20europe%202016.pdf.

16 Sarah Spencer and Vanessa Hughes (July 2015), "Outside and In: Legal Entitlements to Health Care and Education for Migrants with Irregular Status in Europe", COMPAS, Oxford University.

17 See IOM (2016), op. cit. note 21, at 38–40.

18 Centre for Reproductive Rights (CRR), National Latina Institute for Reproductive Health (2013), "Nuestro Texas: The Fight for Women's Reproductive Health in the Rio Grande Valley".

19 See, e.g., PICUM (2017), "Cities of Rights: Ensuring Health Care for Undocumented Residents", at 25.

20 J. Simon, N. Kiss, A. Łaszewska, and S. Mayer (2015), "Public Health Aspects of Migrant Health: A Review of the Evidence on Health Status for Labour Migrants in the European Region", WHO Health Evidence Network (HEN).

21 IOM (September 2016), "Recommendations on Access to Health Services for Migrants in an Irregular Situation".

22 Marc B. Schenker (2010), "A Global Perspective on Migration and Occupational Health", *American Journal of Industrial Medicine*, 53(4): 329–337.

23 European Agency for Safety and Health and Work (2014), "Occupational Health and Safety in the Hairdressing Sector".

24 Sarah Maslin Nir, "Perfect Nails, Poisoned Workers", *New York Times*, 8 May 2015. See also A. Triandafyllidou (2013), *Irregular Migrant Domestic Workers in Europe: Who Cares?* London: Routledge.

25 International Labour Organisation (ILO), Research Series: Global Action Programme on Migrant Domestic Workers and their Families, "Migrant Domestic Workers: Promoting Occupational Safety and Health".

26 Core components of the EU's migration policy include the scaled-up use of detention as a tool for supporting increased numbers of deportations; integrating this deterrence-oriented policy into agreements with third countries, including by using humanitarian assistance as a lever for a state's agreement to accept people deported from the EU; and tackling smuggling, including by partnering with the Libyan border and coastguard to deter transit from Libya to Europe. See, e.g., the EU's action plan on return.

27 European Commission First VP Frans Timmermans, Press Release (8 December 2016), "Commission Reports Progress Made Under the European Agenda on Migrations", Brussels.

28 International Organisation for Migration (IOM) (2016), "Fatal Journeys: Tracking Lives Lost During Migration".

29 MSF (March 2017), "One Year On From the EU-Turkey Deal: Challenging the EU's Alternative Facts".

30 EMN (2014), "The Use of Detention and Alternatives to Detention in the Context of Immigration Policies", Synthesis report for the EMN focussed study 2014.

31 T. Filges, E. Montgomery, M. Kastrup, and A-M. Klint Jørgensen (September 2015), "The Impact of Detention on the Health of Asylum Seekers: A Systematic Review", Campbell Collaboration, https://campbellcollaboration.org/library/impact-of-detention-on-the-health-of-asylum-seekers.html.

32 S. E. Zimmerman, D. Chatty, and M. L. Norredam (2012), "Health Needs and Access to Care in Immigration Detention: Perceptions of Former Detainees", *International Journal of Migration Health and Social Care*, 8(4): 180–185. See also PICUM Bulletin (September 2015), "Migrant Women File Complaint over Lack of Medical Care in Family Detention Centres", http://picum.org/en/news/bulletins/48295/#cat_25446.

33 S. Mares and J. Jureidini (December 2004), "Psychiatric Assessment of Children and Families in Immigration Detention – Clinical, Administrative and Ethical Issues", *Australian and New Zealand Journal of Public Health*, 28(6): 520–526; K. Brabeck and Q. Xu (July 2010), "The Impact of Detention and Deportation on Latino Immigration Children and Families: A Quantitative Exploration", *Hispanic Journal of Behavioral Sciences*, 32(3): 341–361.

34 A. Lorek, K. Ehntholt, A. Nesbitt, and R. Wickramasinghe (2009), "The Mental and Physical Health Difficulties of Children Held Within a British Immigration Detention Centre: A Pilot Study", *Child Abuse and Neglect*, 33: 573–585.

35 Intercollege briefing paper (2009), "Significant Harm: The Effects of Administrative Detention on the Health of Children, Young People and Their Families".

36 "The Arrest and Detention of Children Subject to Immigration Control", a report following the Children's Commissioner to England's visit to Yarl's Wood Immigration Removal Centre (2009).

37 Medical Justice (2011), "Detained and Denied: The Clinic Care of Immigration Detainees Living with HIV".

38 About the role of cities, see PICUM (2017), op. cit. note 19; for a discussion about the role of health professionals, see PICUM (2016), op. cit. note 10, at 18.

7 Migrant risks and insurance

Aparna Dalal and Craig Churchill

Risks and insurance for migrants

Migration is a risk mitigation strategy. Migration allows families to seek higher incomes, diversify their sources of income or escape crisis situations. Migrants often bear the burden of risks of their families and provide informal insurance in the form of remittances during emergencies. Research indicates that migrants that are risk averse are more likely to send remittances home and are, on average, likely to remit a higher amount.[1]

While migrants offer protection to their families, they are often themselves unprotected as they may be ineligible to, or be unaware of how to, access the health services or social safety net programmes of their host countries because of their immigration status[2] or because they work in the informal sector. They face multiple risks, including unsafe working conditions and unstable or under-employment. Financial institutions often do not cater to the needs of migrants, leading to limited access to social, financial and legal services. Smaller social networks in host countries mean that migrants are not able to tap into informal insurance arrangements (e.g. savings groups, funeral societies) that may be accessible to local groups in the same socio-economic strata. These risks and limited ability to manage them pose an economic burden on migrants and their families and make it difficult for migrants to cope with emergencies, thereby making them and their families more vulnerable.

Not all migrants are the same.[3] Global estimates on migrant workers found 230 million international migrants and 150 migrant workers. Migrants that are escaping from a crisis situation require different protection for themselves and their families than those seeking better economic opportunities. The act of migration itself can create additional risks because of the up-front investment needed[4] and increased vulnerability because of being in new surroundings. In some migration corridors, costs are equivalent to only a few days of work (e.g. from Bulgaria to Spain), while in other corridors costs can be as high as ten months of work (e.g. from Pakistan to Saudi Arabia).[5] Migration can also lead to increased vulnerability for the migrant's family because of the absence of one of its members;[6] and families may be less willing to seek alternate sources of income.[7]

The type of risk management solutions needed vary depending on the migrant's context and the stage of their migration journey. Market-based insurance solutions that target migrants can offer risk protection to both migrants and families and fill the gap created because of limited access to social safety nets and informal insurance mechanisms. The unique risks and circumstances facing migrants and their families mean that insurers need to carefully design products and operations. Migration-linked insurance products can cover risks faced by migrants in their host countries (such as accident, death or illness) and risks faced by families in their home countries (such as illness or asset loss). Products may provide benefits for both the migrant and the family, especially in cases where a risk event affects the migrant's ability to send remittances home and worsens the economic wellbeing of their families. Finally, insurance that covers repatriation costs in the unfortunate death of a migrant is important for families.

Insurance providers have found it difficult to penetrate this untapped market segment due to a number of challenges, including lack of understanding on the part of the insurers about the risks faced, difficulty in marketing to migrants or their families, regulatory restrictions and lack of a cost-effective aggregator or distribution channels. These operational challenges make it more expensive for insurers to target migrants and their families.

Migrant-focused insurance solutions broadly fall into three models (see Figure 7.1).[8] The models differ based on the location of the insurer, whether the insured is the migrant or the migrant family, the type of risks covered and the distribution channels involved.

1 Home country model: In this model the insurer is located in the migrant's country of origin. The insured can be the migrant and/or the migrant's family. If the migrant is the insured, the policy is typically sold at the start of the migrant journey before the migrant leaves. In some instances, government mandates that migrants purchase insurance before their departure. Families can buy policies to cover their risks or a risk facing the migrant (such as death or unemployment) that may in turn affect the families' economic position.
2 Host country model: In this model the insurer is located in the country that the migrant has migrated to. Products typically cover risks related

to death, accident, illness or property loss. Host programmes do not insure the migrant's family in the home country due to regulatory and geographic barriers related to marketing, enrolment and claims processing. However, the insurance product can include benefits that are payable to the migrant's family, such as payment in the case of death of the migrant.

3 Hybrid model: The hybrid model includes schemes where the insurer has a presence in both the home and the host country, allowing the insurer to cover both the migrant and their family. Hybrid models may also facilitate the provision of cross-border insurance products, whereby the migrant in the host country can directly pay for a policy (perhaps linked to remittance) insuring the migrant's family at home. Legal and regulatory restrictions pose the biggest challenge to hybrid models as insurers (except for large multinationals) are not licensed in both the home and the host country.

Expanding access: challenges and solutions

Selling microinsurance on a voluntary basis to individuals has proven to be challenging owing to a number of factors, such as low awareness of insurance, lack of trust, poor understanding on insurers' part of the needs of clients and challenges in finding an appropriate distribution channel. These challenges become more critical in the case of migrants because of bi-localization of the target market and the need for payments and services to be provided across borders. Migration-linked microinsurance schemes must either find a way to market to both sides of the transnational family or structure their programme in such a way that one party has full decision-making power.[9]

Consumer education for trust

Special attention needs to be paid to consumer education for migrants' families as they may not have had exposure to formal insurance products. Personalized attention and education are key to building trust and stimulating demand but it is important to frame the messages to appeal to the perceptions of the migrants, as depicted by the case of Seguros Futuro in El Salvador. Seguros Futuro provides a repatriation and remittance insurance product, which covers the full cost of preparing and repatriating the body of a migrant relative should he/she die while in the United States or Canada. The product is offered to the receivers of remittances, who decide whether to insure their migrant family members.

Personalized dialogue proved important to build trust. The majority of cooperative clients surveyed who purchased the product cited conversations

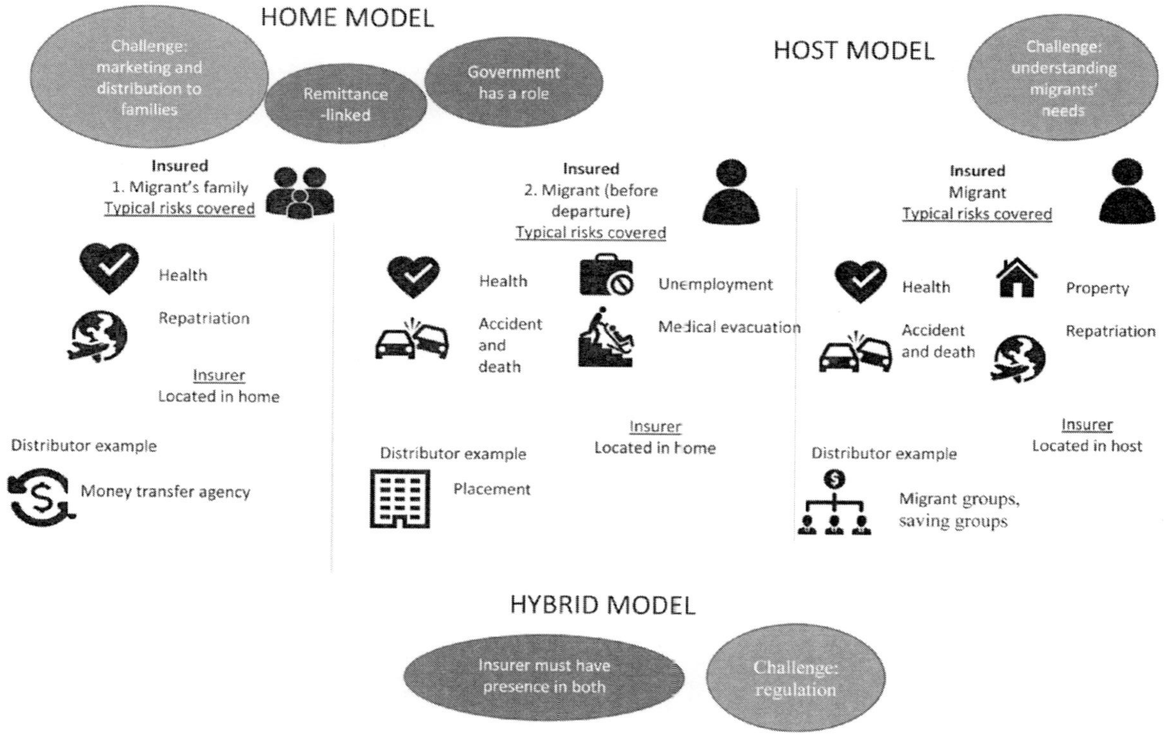

Figure 7.1 Three insurance models.

with Seguros Futuro staff (54 per cent), cooperative staff (20 per cent) or financial education (22 per cent) as their primary motivation. By contrast, no clients mentioned marketing materials (flyers, brochures, banners) as a motivation for purchasing, and radio, loudspeaker and television ads convinced few clients to purchase insurance. Seguros Futuro also found that the nature of the relationship between the sender and receiver of remittances influences the decision to buy insurance. In interviews and surveys with receivers as well as cooperative staff, Seguros Futuro discovered that remittance receivers perceive their migrant family members as 'people to be grateful to' (parents or spouses) and 'people to protect' (sons and daughters); and remittance receivers are almost three times more likely to purchase insurance for 'people to protect'.

Marketing to migrants

The experience of practitioners suggests that it may be more effective to market insurance to migrants, rather than to their families, because the spending and risk management preferences differ. Typically, migrants' families decide how to spend remittances, often choosing to spend most of the money on consumption and basic household needs. Even when they have remittances that are sufficient, families may be unlikely to purchase insurance, since having family members abroad may be perceived as an informal form of insurance, and remittance received seen as a substitute for insurance. Migrants may be more interested in purchasing insurance for their families both to protect their families and to avoid bearing unplanned and potentially catastrophic costs in the case of a crisis. Studies reviewed in the paper indicate that, if given full control over how remittances are spent, migrants and their families would spend money very differently, with migrants allocating less to daily consumption and more to savings. One survey found that migrants were interested in transferring some of their risks and family responsibilities to more formal channels, such as insurance.

Link to remittance flows

Migrant-linked insurance products provide an opportunity for insurers and related stakeholders, especially if providers can tap into the large remittance flow by linking or embedding insurance with remittances. Remittances sent home by international migrants from developing countries were estimated at $432 billion in 2015.[10] SegurCaixa, an affiliate of La Caixa, one of the largest cooperatives in Spain, offers one of the few migration-linked insurance products to reach scale. In 2008, 66,000 legal migrants, mostly from Africa and Latin America, were insured with SegurCaixa Repatriación and 14,000 were covered by SegurIngreso. SegurCaixa Repatriación pays a sum upon the death of the migrant and covers the repatriation of the migrant's body to his or her country of origin, as well as travel expenses for a family member or friend. Through SegurIngreso, beneficiaries receive a payment as well as regular monthly income for five years in the event of the migrant's death.

Distribution partnerships

Partnerships with remittance companies and other players such as migrant associations, church groups or financial institutions can be an effective strategy to overcome marketing and sales challenges and lower operational costs. Further, bundling insurance with other financial services such as savings can offer more value to the migrant and their families through better risk management. Linking insurance to savings promotes asset building, overcomes liquidity constraints and helps to create trust as clients can more easily gain experience of financial services. In the Philippines, Pioneer Life offered a bundled savings and life and accident cover to families of migrant workers. The product was offered through savers and wellness clubs in schools and churches and Pioneer conducted an extensive financial literacy campaign to encourage a culture of saving.

Tackling regulation

Regulatory restrictions pose one of the most significant constraints to selling insurance to migrants because insurance companies may not have a legal presence in either the home or the host countries. Insurance companies in the home country of the migrant find it difficult (and often are not legally allowed) to market to migrants in the host countries. To overcome the regulatory burdens and difficulties in marketing to migrants once they move to the host country, one idea is to offer insurance before migrants leave their home country, and governments can play an important role here.

Governments can use a combination of regulation and partnerships to ensure that migrant workers have access to protection in their host countries. In Indonesia, approximately 90–95 per cent of migrants use a placement agency to arrange their work visas, travel and employment abroad. As of 2006, all placement agencies are mandated to provide migrants with a composite insurance product that provides protection prior to the migrant's departure, during their stay in the host country and upon their return. Packages can cover accidental death or disability, death from sickness, funeral costs, medical expenses, trip cancellation, physical abuse, failure in work placement, early contract termination, unpaid wages, deportation, mental illness, unauthorized work transfer, and legal and court fees. The insurance is distributed by migrant placement agencies, but the protection is provided by private insurers.[11] Similarly, in the Philippines, the Agency-Hired Overseas Filipino Workers (OFW) Compulsory Insurance is an insurance mechanism made available by law to provide insurance protection for Filipino migrant workers. All agency-hired overseas workers are mandated to buy insurance (sponsored by the agency) that covers death, accident, permanent disability and repatriation cover. The insurance is mandated by law and provided by private insurers.

Conclusion

Insurance, if designed properly, can address the unique risk management needs of migrants. Providers must decide which model is best suited given the prevailing regulation, the need for marketing and consumer education, and the availability of distribution partners and technology for operations (such as cross-border finance solutions). It is important that the insurance solution is designed to address the priority risks of migrants and their families as it will be challenging to provide a comprehensive solution from the start. Rather, as trust and knowledge among clients increase and as experience of providers grows, providers can gradually offer greater protection to a wider number of migrants.

Notes

1 Batista, C. and Umblijs, J. 2015, ‘Do Migrants Send Remittances as a Way of Self-Insurance? Evidence from a Representative Immigrant Survey’, IZA Discussion Paper No. 7984.

2 Tangcharoensathien, V., Thwin, A. and Patcharanarumol, W. 2017, ‘Implementing Health Insurance for Migrants, Thailand’, Bulletin World Health Organization No. 95.

3 International Labour Organization (ILO) 2015, ‘ILO Global Estimates on Migrant Workers: Results and Methodology – Special Focus on Migrant Domestic Workers’, available at: www.ilo.org/global/topics/labour-migration/publications/WCMS_436343/lang--en/index.htm (accessed 10 January 2018).

4 Overcoming the difficulties faced by migrant workers and their families with respect to social security coverage is an important challenge that needs to be addressed urgently. The ILO is mandated to extend social security to all in need of such protection, as embedded in the Declaration of Philadelphia (1944) and recently reaffirmed in the Social Protection Floors Recommendation, 2012 (No. 202), and its resolution. For more information on the standards, see www.ilo.org/wcmsp5/groups/public/---ed_protect/---protrav/---migrant/documents/publication/wcms_384861.pdf.

5 Global Forum on Migration and Development (GFMD) 2016, 'Reducing Migration Costs', Background paper for Roundtable 1.1.
6 Gilmer, I. and Riester, A. 2010, 'Microinsurance and Remittances – Teaming Up for Development or Living in Different Worlds?', Discussion Paper: Remittances and Microinsurance, German Technical Cooperation (GIZ).
7 Chen, J. 2006, 'Migration and Imperfect Monitoring: Implications for Intra-Household Allocation'. *American Economic Review*, 96(2): 227–231.
8 Powers, J., Magnoni, B. and Zimmerman, E. 2011, 'Formalizing the Informal Insurance Inherent in Migration', ILO's Impact Insurance Facility Microinsurance Paper No. 10.
9 Idem.
10 World Bank 2016, 'Migration and Development', Brief No. 26.
11 World Bank 2010, 'Enhancing Access to Finance for Indonesian Overseas Migrant Workers: Evidence from a Survey of Three Provinces', Working Paper Volume 2; Powers, J., Magnoni, B. and Zimmerman, E. 2011, 'Formalizing the Informal Insurance Inherent in Migration', ILO's Impact Insurance Facility Microinsurance Paper No. 10.

8 The criminalisation of irregular migrants

Valsamis Mitsilegas and Yewa S. Holiday

Introduction

The criminalisation of migration has been addressed within wider analyses of the link between migration and 'illegality'[1] as well as the process of securitisation of migration and its legal implications.[2] In the US, Legomsky has identified the importing of criminal law enforcement strategies in the field of immigration control with the use of the criminal law to punish immigration violations combined with immigration law consequences, such as expulsion, to criminal convictions.[3]

The European perspective, which has been described as embracing 'a much broader understanding' of criminalisation,[4] includes adverse consequences for migrants in terms of residence and employment rights,[5] the relationship between the use of the substantive criminal law and European Union Law[6] and fundamental principles of criminal law.[7] This contrasts with the Asia Pacific region, where irregular migration is seen through the lens of security and sovereignty at the expense of workers' rights;[8] and Africa, where, on the one hand, criminalisation is fuelled by xenophobia in countries such as South Africa[9] and on the other, criminalisation has been heavily influenced by European concerns in West African countries such as Senegal.[10] South America, however, seems less disposed to criminalisation due perhaps to a more liberal outlook.[11]

The analysis focuses on the global situation using the UK as a case study. The UK has developed one of the most far-reaching and multi-layered criminalisation regimes in the western world.[12] This exacerbates the migrant premium as irregular migrants are increasingly pushed to the margins of society as security concerns are elevated over the rights of migrants.

Criminalisation of irregular entry and residence

Migrants may irregularly migrate in various ways,[13] which may be summarised as irregular entry and residence. This reflects the categorisation in international refugee law where article 31(1) of the Refugee Convention prohibits the penalisation of refugees for offences relating to 'unlawful entry and stay'.[14] The Smuggling Protocol also includes a non-penalisation clause for irregular migrants (article 5) who have been smuggled (articles 5, 6(1)(a)) using fraudulent travel or identity documents (article 6(1)(b)) and/or who have been assisted by a smuggler to remain (article 6(1)(c)). While the Trafficking Protocol recognises that victims of human trafficking may cross borders with false travel documents or without documents (article 10(1)(a)), unlike the Refugee Convention or the Smuggling Protocol, it does not include a non-penalisation clause.

Regional non-penalisation clauses include article 26 of the Council of Europe Convention on Action against Trafficking in Human Beings and article 8 of the European Union (EU)'s Directive 2011/36/EU (Human Trafficking). However, these invite prosecutors not to criminalise rather than requiring non-criminalisation. Unlike, the European Union, the African Union has produced guidelines which provide for the exemption of penalties for asylum-seekers.[15] Legislation exists exempting refugees from offences of unlawful entry and presence – for example, in Africa,[16] the Americas,[17] Asia[18] and Europe[19] – and over 50 per cent of countries have enacted anti-trafficking legislation.[20] However, most irregular migrants globally are not asylum-seekers or trafficked and may fall foul of legislation criminalising irregular entry and stay.

The Court of Justice of the European Union (CJEU) has held that the terms of the Returns Directive,[21] which applies to 'illegally' staying 'third country nationals', must be interpreted in order to return irregular migrants to their state of origin rather than criminalise them.[22] Nevertheless, most countries in Europe have legislation which criminalises migrants for irregular entry or stay[23] – for example, France, Italy, Germany and the Netherlands.[24] Germany, the Netherlands and Spain criminalise irregular stay (Italy has reverted to an administrative penalty[25]). The Netherlands criminalises irregular stay in circumstances where the migrant has been declared an 'undesirable alien' or has failed to comply with an order to leave the Netherlands.[26] While Italy and Spain only provide for fines, the others provide for custodial sentences.

The UK has a range of offences in immigration and non-immigration law which criminalise irregular entry and stay. Offences may relate to irregular entry – such as using false ID documents or documents belonging to others (section 26(1)(d) Immigration Act (IA) 1971; sections 4 and 6

Identity Documents Act (IDA) 2010), entering in breach of a deportation order (section 24(1)(a) IA 1971), seeking leave to enter or remain (section 24A IA 1971), failing to produce a passport (section 2 Asylum and Immigration (Treatment of Claimant's) Act 2004) – or breach of leave conditions, such as overstaying (sections 24(1)(b)(i) and 24(1)(c) IA 1971) – or relate to the state's attempts to expel the migrant (section 35, AI(TC) A, which criminalises failed asylum-seekers who refuse to cooperate in their removal from the UK) – or otherwise to 'disrupt the day-to-day activities' of migrants present in the UK in irregular ways (for example, driving when not lawfully resident in the UK, section 24C IA 1971).[27] They attract penalties of a fine and/or maximum sentences of imprisonment between six months in the lower courts and ten years in the Crown Courts.

Irregular migration has tended to be analysed in Europe and America but not in countries of origin such as West Africa.[28] In Senegal, the analysis of legal decisions 'adopted in a climate of heavy national and international political pressure' reveals the criminalisation of irregular migration before it has even occurred.[29] The data analysed showed a high rate of prosecution (97 per cent) of Senegalese nationals for 'unlawful migration', 'unlawful immigration',[30] unlawful emigration'[31] and 'unlawful embarkation'.[32] The law was derived from the Smuggling and Trafficking Protocols. These various terms described the same phenomenon: mostly Senegalese citizens who had left Senegal or were leaving Senegal by sea. None of the Senegalese nationals were correctly prosecuted as, being Senegalese, they were not committing any offence by leaving Senegal and they had not crossed any border. Ndiaye and Robin noted that those entering the territory irregularly were not prosecuted but rather administratively expelled. This meant that the 'first criminalization of migrants' in Senegal was applied to its own nationals.[33] The mixing of smugglers and migrants resulted in Senegal treating migration as a legally wrongful act and migrants being treated as criminals. This shows how potential irregular migrants may be criminalised even before they reach a country of destination.

Criminalisation of irregular working

From the perspective of the country of destination, irregular migrant workers cover a range of situations, from those who have a entered a country irregularly and work without permission, to those who entered regularly but do not have the right to work, such as tourists or students, those who do not have a valid work permit and those who have become irregular due to overstaying.[34] Irregularity is thus fluid and may change over time.

Many countries make the employment of irregular migrants a criminal offence punishable with imprisonment and/or fines.[35] Under EU law, Directive 2009/52/EC[36] imposes fines and criminal sanctions against employers who employ irregular migrants and gives irregular workers the right to overdue wages, including the difference between them and the legal minimum wage (article 6).[37] In the US, while there exists legislation criminalising the employment of irregular migrants (the Immigration, Reform and Control Act 1986), this is not generally enforced.[38]

However, penalties are more common against irregular migrant workers than their employers. For example, in the Asian-Pacific region, irregular migrant workers are subject to arrest, detention and deportation.[39] In Thailand, irregular migrants and their employers make informal payments to local authorities to avoid deportation, with migrants referred to as 'walking ATMs' and a major source of income.[40] In Malaysia, irregular migrants are held in police custody, prisons and detention until deportation. Those who work without a valid work permit in Singapore face a fine of up to $20,000, two years' imprisonment, or both, and may also be barred from entry to the country for a period of time.[41] Victnam has introduced penalties against irregular migrants following a temporary ban on migrants from Vietnam entering the Republic of Korea due to a high rate of overstays. Migrant workers from Vietnam who abscond from their employers face fines of about $3,800–$4,700.

The UK has made working by an irregular migrant a crime in itself. This is part of the UK's expansion of the criminalisation of migration generally, exemplified by the battery of measures in its Immigration Acts of 2014 and 2016, such as seizure of driving licences, impounding of vehicles,[42] disqualification from renting private premises,[43] closing of bank accounts and seizure of assets,[44] broadening sanctions against employers,[45] as well as criminal offences.

In the UK, there are two ways of criminalising migrants who work in an irregular way, either by breaching a condition relating to their 'employment or occupation' (section 24(1)(e) IA 1971) or via an 'illegal working' offence[46] applicable to those who enter the UK irregularly or overstay their leave (section 24B IA 1971, as amended by the IA 2016). The concept of 'working' in the latter offence is very broad (24B(10)(a)–(e)) and is intended to include 'informal arrangements that have no paperwork or contract'.[47] The sanction for these offences is a fine and/or a maximum of six months' imprisonment.

The IA 2016 also criminalises irregular migrants who work in licensed premises[48] and hold taxi and private hire driver and operator licences[49] and prevents irregular migrants from obtaining a personal or premises licence to sell alcohol.[50] A migrant who has such a licence will be working irregularly and will therefore be committing an offence under section 24 IA 1971.[51]

Irregular migrants may also breach offences in criminal legislation, for example, where the work is unlawful per se (as where a migrant is forced to grow cannabis[52] where the unlawfulness lies in both the coercive nature [slavery/trafficking] and the fact that growing cannabis is illegal) or where false identity documents are used to try to obtain work.[53]

The migrant premium

The criminalisation of irregular migrants has the potential to worsen the situation of the irregular migrant worker. While few irregular migrants are prosecuted for the way in which they enter or reside,[54] inability to work in lawful ways makes it difficult for them to earn, save money and send it abroad.

The only jobs open to irregular migrants are those where the conditions are poor (for example, low wages or enforced work, such as trafficking or slavery).[55] They may then become enmeshed in the black market and may be at risk from smugglers and traffickers.[56] This increases the migrant premium and makes it more difficult to obtain earnings to send abroad.

The situation of the irregular migrant faced with these measures and offences reveals a disregard for international norms[57] which tend to separate the human and working rights of irregular migrants[58] from questions about immigration status. Provisions protecting irregular migrant workers include article 9, MWC 1975 (right to equal treatment and to work for irregular migrants) and article 15, MWC 1990 (migrant workers should not 'be arbitrarily deprived of property' without 'the right to fair and adequate compensation').[59] Other international and regional norms include articles 6 and 7 of the ICESCR, which protect the right to work under favourable conditions; articles 7, 8 and 10 of the ICCPR and articles 3, 4 and 5 of the ECHR, which prohibit torture, slavery and protect the right to liberty, respectively;[60] and article 24 of the ICESCR and article 14 of the ICCPR, which provide for non-discrimination before the law. In Asia, the Association of Southeast Asian Nations (ASEAN) adopted the Declaration on the Protection and Promotion of the Rights of Migrant Workers ('the Cebu Declaration') in 2007. However, protecting irregular migrant workers remains a block to the drafting of a regional instrument realising the principles outlined in the Cebu Declaration.[61] For example, Malaysia and Thailand are opposed to protections for irregular migrant workers because they consider that this would undermine regular migration.[62]

The ability of low-skilled irregular migrants to access justice is restricted. In the UK context, for example, section 45 of the Modern

Slavery Act provides a defence for victims of slavery and human trafficking who have been compelled to commit an offence[63] as a direct consequence of their situation so that they are not 'inappropriately prosecuted or convicted'.[64] However, criminalising work undermines this as the new offence could make it more difficult for victims of trafficking to seek help. Irregular migrants who are not enslaved or trafficked have little redress as the defence of illegality is generally fatal to an irregular worker's claim.[65]

Globally, migrants are exposed to fines, imprisonment and deportation or removal for the manner in which they enter or reside. The irregularity of their status also makes it difficult for them to work as they are in a 'legally isolated space' which weakens their 'ability to assert their rights'.[66] This criminalisation of migrants has the effect of exacerbating the migrant premium as it puts migrants at risk of imprisonment, loss of wages, confiscation and potential subsequent deportation. This decreases income and any surplus available for investment, increases dependency on employers, smugglers and traffickers and complicates access to human rights protection. What irregular migrants require is the flexibility to manage their affairs, not criminalisation.

Notes

1 Catherine Dauvergne, *Making People Illegal What Globalisation Means for Migration and Law* (CUP 2008).

2 E.g. Jennifer M. Chacon, 'Unsecured Borders: Immigration Restrictions, Crime Control and National Security' (2007) 39 Connecticut Law Review 1827; Valsamis Mitsilegas, 'Immigration Control in an Era of Globalisation: Deflecting Foreigners, Weakening Citizens, Strengthening the State' (2012) 19 Indiana Journal of Global Legal Studies 3.

3 Stephen H. Legomsky, 'The New Path of Immigration Law: Asymmetric Incorporation of Criminal Justice Norms' (2007) 64 Washington and Lee Law Review 469; see also Juliet P. Stumpf, 'The Crimmigration Crisis: Immigrants, Crime and Sovereign Power' (2006) 56 American University Law Review 367; Juliet P. Stumpf, 'The Process Is the Punishment in Crimmigration Law' in Katja Franko Aas and Mary Bosworth (eds), *The Borders of Punishment: Migration, Citizenship and Social Exclusion* (OUP 2013).

4 Mark Provera, 'The Criminalisation of Irregular Migration in the European Union' (2015) 80 CEPS Paper in Liberty and Security in Europe 4.

5 Elspeth Guild, *Criminalisation* (Council of Europe Commissioner for Human Rights 2009).

6 Valsamis Mitsilegas, 'The Changing Landscape of the Criminalisation of Migration in Europe. The Protective Function of European Union Law' in Maria Joao Guia, Maartje Van der Woude and Joanne van der Leun (eds), *Social Control and Justice: Crimmigration in an Age of Fear* (Eleven International Publishing 2012); Valsamis Mitsilegas, *The Criminalisation of Migrants in Europe. Challenges for Human Rights and the Rule of Law* (Springer 2014).

7 Alessandro Spena, 'Iniuria Migrandi: Criminalization of Immigrants and the Basic Principles of the Criminal Law' (2014) 8 Criminal Law and Philosophy 635; Alessandro Spena, 'A Just Criminalization of Irregular Immigration: Is It Possible?' [2015] Criminal Law and Philosophy 1.

8 Melissa Curley and Siu-Iun Wong, *Security and Migration in Asia* (Routledge 2008); Migrant Forum in Asia, *Compilation of Reports on the Detention of Undocumented Migrants* (Migrants Rights International 2012); Nicholas Henry, *Asylum, Work and Precarity: Bordering the Asia-Pacific* (Springer 2017); Max Tunon and Benjamin Harkins, 'Addressing Irregular Migration and Violations of Migrant Workers' Rights' in Jean-Christophe Dumont and others (eds), *Safeguarding the Rights of Asia Migrant Workers from Home to the Workplace* (ILO 2017).

9 Theresa Alfaro-Velcamp and Mark Shaw, '"Please GO HOME and BUILD Africa": Criminalising Immigrants in South Africa' (2016) 42 Journal of Southern African Studies 983.

10 Mandiogou Ndiaye and Nelly Robin, 'Migrants Criminalised While Making the Journey' in OECD, Sahel and West Africa Club (ed.), *West African Studies Regional Challenges of West African Migration African and European Perspectives* (OECD Publishing 2009).

11 David Cantor, Luisa Feline Freier and Pierre Jean, 'Introduction: A Paradigm Shift in Latin American Immigration and Asylum Law and Policy?', *A Liberal Tide? Immigration and Asylum Law and Policy in Latin America* (SAS 2015).

12 Other regimes include Europe, Mitsilegas, *The Criminalisation of Migrants in Europe. Challenges for Human Rights and the Rule of Law* (n 6); Provera (n 4); the US, Stumpf, 'The Crimmigration Crisis: Immigrants, Crime and Sovereign Power' (n 3); and Asia, Henry (n 8).

13 F. Düvell, 'Paths into Irregularity: The Legal and Political Construction of Irregular Migration' (2011) 13 European Journal of Migration and Law 275.

14 Cathryn Costello, *Article 31 of the 1951 Convention Relating to the Status of Refugees* (UNHCR Division of International Protection 2017); Guy S. Goodwin-Gill, 'Article 31' in Erika Feller, Volker Turk and Frances Nicholson (eds), *Refugee Protection in International Law* (CUP 2003).

15 OAU Guidelines for National Refugee Legislation and Commentary, adopted by OAU/UNHCR Working Group on Arusha Follow-up Second Meetings, 4–5 December 1980, Part IV (1) and (2) in Goodwin-Gill (n 14) 252.

16 Costello (n 14); E.g. Goodwin-Gill (n 14) 199–201, 244, 251–52; Nigeria, Decree of 1989, National Commission for Refugees, s 1; South Africa, Act No 130 of 1998, ss 3, 22.

17 S 10(1) Belize, Refugees Act 1991; Goodwin-Gill (n 14) 198–99; arts 8, 10, Brazil Law No 9474 of 1997; s 133, Canada, Immigration and Refugee Protection Act 2001.

18 Art 3, Turkmenistan Law of Refugees 1997, Goodwin-Gill (n 14) 247.

19 Ibid. (Switzerland, Finland, Spain), 197–99; s 31, Immigration and Asylum Act 1999, UK.

20 See Human Trafficking Knowledge Portal at www.unodc.org/unodc/en/human-trafficking/index.html?ref=menuside.

21 'Directive 2002/90/EC on the Facilitation of Unauthorised Entry, Transit and Residence, OJ L 328, 28/11/2002' 90.

22 See also Mitsilegas, *The Criminalisation of Migrants in Europe. Challenges for Human Rights and the Rule of Law* (n 6), 57–75.

23 Provera (n 4); EU Agency for Fundamental Rights, *Criminalisation of Migrants in an Irregular Situation and of Persons Engaging with Them* (EU FRA 2014).
24 Provera (n 4), 16.
25 Spena, 'Iniuria Migrandi: Criminalization of Immigrants and the Basic Principles of the Criminal Law' (n 7).
26 Provera (n 4).
27 This offence is not yet in force. A migrant, disqualified from driving under s 37 IA 2016, who fails to return the licence within seven days without reasonable cause, commits an offence. The penalty is a fine which continues on a daily basis for every day the documents are not returned after conviction.
28 Ndiaye and Robin (n 10).
29 Ibid., 177.
30 Ninety-six per cent were Senegalese nationals, ibid., 181.
31 Seventy-two per cent were Senegalese, ibid., 181–82.
32 Ninety-three per cent were Senegalese, ibid., 182.
33 Ibid., 187–88.
34 Tunon and Harkins (n 8), 44.
35 For the Asia region, see ibid.; Maria Segrave, 'What It's Like to Live and Work Illegally in Australia' https://theconversation.com/what-its-like-to-live-and-work-illegally-in-australia-81478; for Europe, see Provera (n 4).
36 This is not implemented by the UK, Ireland or Denmark.
37 Provera (n 4), 18.
38 'Editorial, No Crackdown on Illegal Employers' *New York Times* (20 March 2017).
39 Tunon and Harkins (n 8).
40 Ibid., 54.
41 Ibid.
42 Ss 24D-F, IA 1971.
43 Ss 21, 22 IA 2014.
44 S 40 IA 2014.
45 Ss 35, 38 IA 2016.
46 The offence is described thus in the legislation.
47 S 24B(13).
48 S 36 amends Schedule 4 of the Licensing Act 2003.
49 In force 1 December 2016.
50 S 36.
51 S 8A(8) Metropolitan Carriage Act 1869, as amended.
52 Production and cultivation of cannabis contrary to ss 4 and 6 Misuse of Drugs Act ('MDA') 1971.
53 Offences under ss 4 and 6, IDA 2010.
54 Most migrants who enter the UK irregularly will be removed rather than prosecuted, Ana Aliverti, *Immigration Offences: Trends in Legislation and Criminal and Civil Enforcement* (Migration Observatory 2016).
55 See Alice Bloch, Leena Kumarappan and Sonia Mckay, 'Employer Sanctions: The Impact of Workplace Raids and Fines on Undocumented Migrants and Ethnic Enclave Employers' (2015) 35 Critical Social Policy, for the effects in the UK on low-skilled migrants who are caught up in immigration raids and are subsequently detained and/or deported, 133–34, 137.
56 Sonia Pereira and Joao Vasconcelos, *Human Trafficking and Forced Labour* (ILO 2008).

57 ACL Davies, 'The Immigration Act 2016' [2016] ILJ 431 439.
58 ILO Convention 143, art 1. S 24B conflicts with art 9.
59 Migrant Workers Convention. Art 25 provides for equal treatment. See also arts 14, 26 ICCPR, arts 6, 7 CESCR and SDG 8.8.
60 See also *OOO v The Commissioner of Police for the Metropolis* [2011] EWHC 1246 QB; *CN v UK (4239/08)* [2012] ECHR 1911 13 November 2012.
61 Tunon and Harkins (n 8), 43.
62 Ibid.
63 The defence does not apply to certain serious offences such as murder, torture, false imprisonment and robbery.
64 'Public Bill Committee, Immigration Bill, 27 October 2015 (2015–16, HC 189)'; Valsamis Mitsilegas, 'Trafficking: Guidance – Trafficking People Committing Criminal Offences – Correct Approach to Prosecutions' (2011) 5 CLR 425; CPS, *Legal Guidance: Suspects in a Criminal Case Who Might Be Victims of Trafficking or Slavery, Downloaded 4 July 2016* (CPS 2016); see also *LM & Others* [2010] EWCA Crim 2327; *R v L, HVN, THN, T v R, The Children's Commissioner for England and Human Rights Commission* [2013] EWCA Crim 991.
65 In situations where employees are abused or ill-treated, the migrant may bring a discrimination claim, *Hounga v Allen* [2014] UKSC 47.
66 Provera (n 4) 2.

9 Access to justice

Julinda Beqiraj

Access to justice: a definition

The notion of access to justice, entails 'much more than improving an individual's access to courts ... It must be defined in terms of ensuring that legal and judicial outcomes are just and equitable'.[1] An expanded concept of access to justice that covers different stages of the process of obtaining a solution to justice problems is more adequate to understanding and illustrating the migrant premium related to (lack of) effective access to justice. Such a comprehensive approach starts with the existence of rights enshrined in laws, and awareness and understanding of those rights by migrants. It embraces effective access to dispute resolution mechanisms and includes the availability of, and access to, counsel and representation. It also encompasses the ability of such mechanisms to provide just, fair, impartial and enforceable solutions and redress.[2]

We argue that access to justice, despite its own up-front costs, represents an essential tool to mitigate the costs deriving from violations of rights. However, barriers to access to justice narrow the margin of gains (in the form of back payment or compensation) expected from lodging a complaint. The incentives to ask for a remedy are reduced, which perpetuates the rights violations and the related costs suffered by migrants.

Types of violations resulting in costs for migrant workers

Access to justice – as a right and fundamental freedom – is indivisible from and interdependent with other rights. It enables individuals to have their voices heard and to exercise their legal rights and seek redress.

Lack of enforcement of rights results in costs for migrant workers, as discussed in the other chapters in this collection. This is clear in cases concerning underpayment or lack of payment of wages. An expected increase in income when employed abroad is one of the main motivations that drive international labour migration. Defiance of this expectation provides a strong incentive to overcome the fear of reprisal for lodging complaints against employers. A recent ILO study covering South-East Asia reports that wage violations are the most frequent complaints.[3] The study also finds that an important part of these complaints concerned wages below the minimum established by law; these were prompted by the enactment of highly publicised minimum wage legislation.

Other examples of rights violations resulting in direct or indirect costs for migrant workers and their families comprise unsafe working conditions that are harmful to physical and mental health – including where injuries occur for lack of respect of safety requirements; inadequate rest and lack of enjoyment of holidays; physical or sexual abuse, especially for domestic workers; ill-treatment and harassment; and racist hate crimes. Irregular migrants face additional costs in these regards because their irregular status exposes them to enhanced possibilities of violations of rights. Accounts of exploitation, abuse, human trafficking, debt bondage and other severe human rights violations are not unusual.

Access to justice as a tool to reduce the costs of rights violations: opportunities and limits

Access to justice, as a fundamental right in itself and as a precondition of the enjoyment of all other rights, is crucial for migrant workers, as a special category of vulnerable persons, and provides a unique tool to reduce the costs resulting from discrimination, abuse and even violence that they face. Accessing the justice system has its own costs (e.g. fees paid to lawyers, interpreters' and court fees) which nevertheless may be worth paying to obtain remedy and redress for the violation of rights.

Paradoxically, however, those who need effective access to justice most – because the costs resulting from rights violations are high – are the ones most frequently encountering barriers to it. Barriers make the justice process more expensive and reduce the economic value of the expected gains from litigation.

Barriers to access to justice may originate from within and from outside formal justice institutions, and may include societal and cultural barriers, such as literacy, education, language, poverty and discriminatory practices; institutional barriers, such as inadequate organisational structure of justice institutions, limited legal assistance and representation, and lack of enforcement of decisions; and intersectional barriers, where societal and institutional barriers overlap, such as lack of trust in lawyers and judges, and corruption.[4] Below we explain how they affect migrants.

Legal awareness

Knowledge of rights and of available remedies is a precondition to an effective access to justice. On various occasions, the UN bodies monitoring the implementation of human rights obligations have expressed concern about the limited access to justice for migrant workers, due to their lack of awareness of the right to file complaints and obtain effective redress, regardless of status, and of the administrative, judicial and other remedies available to them.[5] Additionally, access to a helpline in a language migrants understand and to interpreters, as well as provision of information regarding possibilities to lodge complaints against those responsible for violence, are essential guarantees for an effective access to justice.[6]

Right to make an application

Where migrants are aware of their rights and the available remedies, access to justice may still be an impracticable solution because of fear of retaliation from the employer or the discriminatory behaviour on the part of the police and other law enforcement officials with whom they lodge a complaint.[7] In the case of irregular migrants, access to justice is further spoiled by monetary fines for carrying out unregistered work, and fear of arrest, detention or deportation due to their status. Moreover, irregular migrant workers who wish to pursue a claim against their employer may be forced to repatriate immediately, once they come clear, without the possibility to access justice.[8] The UN human rights monitoring bodies have often urged states to ensure that all migrants, irrespective of their status, have access to justice and effective remedies, but significant limitations remain in law and practice.[9]

Migrant domestic workers constitute a particularly vulnerable category. The legislation of some countries that provides for employer-tied work permits (e.g. kafala system) contributes to the persistence of abusive practices. Access to justice for domestic workers, mostly women, who live and work in exploitative conditions, is hampered by important obstacles, including fear of expulsion and insecurity of residence while procedures are ongoing.[10] Bringing a claim is likely to mean the end of employment: thus, complaints are an option when life or basic dignity are threatened, but they are not aimed at long-term improvements to wages and working conditions.

According to the ILO study on South-East Asia, a large proportion of surveyed wage payment cases in Thailand were dropped without any form of remedy being obtained, because: (1) complainants discontinued cases due to fears of retaliation; (2) follow-up was not possible because complainants had moved on; and (3) authorities refused to pursue the cases further due to insufficient evidence or lack of legal or procedural requirements (particularly due to the irregular legal status of migrants).[11]

Court fees and costs related to interpretation, legal advice and representation

Lawyer and interpreter services are essential to ensuring effective access to justice for migrants, but these come at a cost. Self-representation, where possible, is less effective for migrants in practice (compared to nationals) because of cultural and linguistic barriers and lack of knowledge of the technical language in legal proceedings.

In many jurisdictions, the law establishes that these services should be provided free of charge – under 'legal aid' – and that court fees should be waived for individuals and households below a certain economic threshold. However, standards differ substantially between countries and access to legal aid may be very restricted in practice. This occurs, for instance, when the legislation in force requires the anticipation of fees and/or makes refund conditional on the success of the claim, and when funding is tightened and restrictive eligibility criteria for legal aid apply, including proof of residence for a certain period in the host country.[12]

Efficiency and quality of justice

The efficiency and quality of the justice system has an impact on the costs related to access to justice. Access to justice for migrants is hindered in practice by delays in the delivery of justice, by the complexity of legal proceedings, by discriminatory treatment in courts and by corruption and abuse of authority.[13] Delays in adjudication often amount to denial of a remedy because migrants may be forced to return home before a resolution has been reached.

Corruption not only hampers the fair resolution of disputes for those that cannot afford the economic costs of bribes but it also – because of the fear of unfairness – discourages individuals from using justice institutions to resolve disputes. While the integrity and independence of judges are vitally important, it is especially at the lower levels, in dealings with administrative staff in everyday contacts, that corruption creates an important barrier to access to justice. Poorly paid staff facilitates corrupt practices and this translates into additional costs for migrants who revert to courts.

Individuals who have been subject to discrimination and abuse by the authorities, or have experienced unjust outcomes from the justice system, notably migrants, may choose not to rely upon legal procedures for the solution of their justice problems. Distrust of the courts is a particularly challenging obstacle because it undermines the chances to resolve disputes within the law – whether between private parties or with public authorities. Cultural barriers also apply. Immigrants may take their concerns about the deficiencies of the justice system in their home jurisdiction and apply them to the justice system of their new host country. The performance of an unfamiliar justice system is not always apparent; therefore, the caution applied in the past is difficult to eradicate.

Types of remedies and enforcement of decisions

Considering the barriers mentioned so far, access to justice becomes cost-efficient for migrant workers only if the remedies obtained, such as reimbursement, financial compensation and damages, can cover the costs related to access to justice and reduce the costs related to rights violations. However, this may prove difficult in practice.

The ILO study conducted in South-East Asia reports that:

> the majority of 'compensation' paid to migrant workers was money owed to them for unpaid wages rather than compensation for harm suffered. It is extremely rare for migrant workers within the region to be awarded additional money in punitive damages for abuse.[14]

Moreover, as highlighted in an EU report:

> it is often very difficult for victims to obtain compensation from offenders, not least because a company that acted as an employer may prefer to declare insolvency or because the responsible individuals disappear. For these reasons, compensation from offenders should be reinforced by state compensation funds.[15]

The lack of adequate remedies or lack of enforcement of decisions is even more critical, in terms of costs, where the death or disappearance of the migrant worker is involved. The UN human rights bodies have exposed such disturbing practices in some countries (e.g. Lebanon, Mexico).[16] Family members may not be in the country where the incident occurred or their irregular status may operate as a barrier to bringing a claim for damages.

The 2030 Sustainable Development Agenda and measurability issues: the prospect of relieving the migrant premium

Most recently, the UN Sustainable Development Goals (SDGs) (officially known as Transforming Our World: The 2030 Agenda for Sustainable Development),[17] where the rule of law and access to justice feature in SDG16, recognise the important interlinkages between access to justice and sustainable development.[18] Under the slogan 'leave no one behind', the Agenda establishes that people who are vulnerable, including refugees and migrants, must be empowered, including through equal access to justice, and acknowledges 'the positive contribution of migrants for inclusive growth and sustainable development'.[19]

The SDGs place strong emphasis on data collection and measurement of progress at global and national levels, including on issues such as: (1) gender inequality (SDG5), (2) decent work, protection of labour rights and promotion of safe working environments for all workers, migrants included, in particular women migrants (SDG8), (3) inequality within states and reduction of transaction costs of migrant remittances (SDG10), and (4) effective access to justice for all (SDG16). Important benefits, in terms of relieving the migrant premium, can be anticipated from an effective implementation of the Agenda; monitoring and assessing the impact of the action undertaken in the context of the SDGs in the coming years will be crucial for at least two reasons.

First, the efforts put in place by states in the collection of data and their breakdown along the relevant categories, such as age, gender, migration status and area (urban/rural), will make available a more accurate confirmation of the additional costs migrant workers incur, when compared to nationals. This will provide an important and strong evidence base for policy reform, which has often been lacking so far. Second, although the SDGs do not specifically use human rights language, nor do they enclose legally enforceable commitments, some of them closely echo the obligations enshrined in human rights instruments concerning migrants' rights. Therefore, data collection will supplement the existing human rights monitoring system with a quantitative measurable dimension of the progress made in the delivery of the Agenda and on its impact on the empowerment of migrants. Better monitoring is expected, ultimately, to improve respect for and protection of human rights standards, and result in a reduction of the costs borne by migrant workers.

Notes

1 United Nations Development Programme (UNDP), Access to Justice: Practice Note, 2004, p. 3.

2 See Julinda Beqiraj and Lawrence McNamara, *Children and Access to Justice: National Practices, International Challenges* (Bingham Centre for the Rule of Law Report 02/2016), International Bar Association, October 2016, p. 5, fn 6.

3 Benjamin Harkins and Meri Åhlberg, *Access to Justice for Migrant Workers in South-East Asia*, International Labour Organization, Bangkok: ILO, 2017.

4 The categorisations we use here are somewhat theoretical and artificial, but they are employed to help situate barriers within wider structures of society, culture and economy, and to capture their complexity. In practice, of course, barriers operate simultaneously and have reciprocal effects on each other that intensify their impact: J. Beqiraj and L. McNamara, *International Access to Justice: Barriers and Solutions* (Bingham Centre for the Rule of Law Report), International Bar Association, October 2014. The different types of obstacles to access to justice encountered by specific groups are pointed out and documented in a number of general comments and recommendations by treaty monitoring bodies, such as: Committee on the Protection of the Rights of All Migrant Workers and Members of Their Families, General comment No. 1 on migrant domestic workers, 2011, General comment No. 2 on the rights of migrant workers in an irregular situation and members of their families, 2013; Committee on the Elimination of Discrimination against Women, General recommendation No. 32 on the gender-related dimensions of refugee status, asylum, nationality and statelessness of women, 2014, and General recommendation No. 33 on women's access to justice, 2015.

5 CMW/C/BLZ/CO/1 (CMW, 2014), CMW/C/PER/CO/1 (CMW, 2015), CMW/C/URY/CO/1 (CMW, 2014), CMW/C/PHL/CO/2 (CMW, 2014).

6 CAT/C/KOR/CO/3–5 (CAT, 2017).

7 CEDAW/C/ARE/CO/2–3 (CEDAW, 2015).

8 A/HRC/32/17 (UPR, 2016) regarding Afghanistan.

9 CERD/C/ITA/CO/19–20 (CERD, 2017), CMW/C/TUR/CO/1 (CMW, 2016).

10 CEDAW/C/LBN/CO/4–5 (CEDAW, 2015).

11 See note 6.

12 CEDAW/C/NZL/CO/7 (CEDAW, 2012), CCPR/C/GBR/CO/7 (CCPR, 2015).

13 A/HRC/4/23/Add.2 (SR Trafficking, 2007) regarding Bahrain, Oman, Qatar; CMW/C/BLZ/CO/1 (CMW, 2014); CEDAW/C/SWE/CO/8–9 (CEDAW, 2016); CEDAW/C/ARE/CO/2–3 (CEDAW, 2015); CMW/C/PHL/CO/2 (CMW, 2014).

14 See note 6.

15 EU Agency for Fundamental Rights, *Severe Labour Exploitation: Workers Moving within or into the European Union*, 2015, p. 21.

16 CEDAW/C/LBN/CO/4–5 (CEDAW, 2015), CED/C/MEX/CO/1 (CED, 2015); Alix Nasri and Wissam Tannous, *Access to Justice for Migrant Domestic Workers in Lebanon*, International Labour Office, Geneva: ILO, 2014, p. 77.

17 A/RES/70/1, Transforming our World: The 2030 Agenda for Sustainable Development, adopted on 25 September 2015 (otherwise known as the 2030 Sustainable Development Agenda).

18 Goal 16 sets out to 'promote peaceful and inclusive societies for sustainable development, provide access to justice for all and build effective, accountable and inclusive institutions at all levels'.

19 2030 Sustainable Development Agenda, para. 29.

10 Migrant incomes, *Big Issue* sellers, penalties and confiscation regimes

Rudi Fortson

On 14 December 2017, the Administrative Court for England and Wales ruled that the 2017 "European Economic Area (EEA) administrative removal"[1] would be quashed insofar as it treated rough sleeping, whether intentional, harmful or otherwise, as an abuse of Treaty rights.[2] The Home Department had contended[3] that EEA rough sleepers did not fulfil the purpose of integration into the host state. In rejecting that contention, the learned judge remarked that she did not consider that rough sleeping "precludes integration in other ways, for example, through work and social ties".[4] However, as this short chapter demonstrates, the receipt by migrants of social benefits or earnings that had been obtained in violation of the criminal law (perhaps by virtue of a migrant's irregular status) can result in financial cost to the migrant in question. Although this "cost" might be viewed as the "just deserts" for an offence committed, there will be cases where a compassionate outcome is warranted and achieved by means other than invoking the criminal justice process.

In June 2014, the United Kingdom's Work and Pensions Secretary (Iain Duncan Smith MP) asserted that "what is happening progressively, more and more, is people mostly from southern and eastern Europe have actually ended up being *Big Issue* sellers and they claim, as self-employed, immediately, tax credits".[5] Three years later, *The Daily Mail* claimed that judges, in a "key judgement", had "cracked down on the scandal of poor EU migrants selling the *Big Issue* as a back door to claiming benefits".[6] In truth, the case in question (*DV v SSWP*)[7] was not a "key judgement" but merely fact and context specific.[8] DV, a Romanian national, came to the UK in January 2015 and began selling the *Big Issue* in April of that year. At that time, an EEA national's "right to reside"[9] in the UK depended (as it does now) on the person being a "qualified person"[10] – an expression that included those who were "self-employed" in the UK "in accordance with article 49 of the [TFEU]".[11] Such work had to be genuine and effective rather than marginal and ancillary.[12] There was no dispute that the First Tier Tribunal had correctly directed itself on the law and it had correctly determined – on the facts – that DV's business was not viable but a means to obtain benefits. DV's employment was, therefore, neither genuine nor effective.[13] The case contrasts with *Bristol City Council v FV*,[14] involving another *Big Issue* seller (a Romanian national) where the Upper Tribunal declined to interfere with the finding *of fact* made at first instance that FV was entitled to certain public funds ("benefits") by reason of being "self-employed" for the purposes of the "right to reside" test. The Upper Tribunal noted that there was nothing in EU law that suggested that selling the *Big Issue* cannot constitute "self-employment".[15] The latter decision, and the Tribunal's reasoning, did not feature in media reports.

As for criminal liability, a wide array of offences exist, carrying terms of imprisonment and/or fines, to punish persons (whether migrants or not) who obtain property unlawfully (including earnings). Prior to the Fraud Act 2006 coming into force,[16] the Theft Act "deception offences"[17] were frequently charged. In *R v Paulet*,[18] P, using a false French passport, earned a gross income of over £73,000. He pleaded guilty to (among other charges) three offences of obtaining a pecuniary advantage by deception (namely, falsely representing that he was entitled to work in the United Kingdom) contrary to s 16 of the Theft Act 1968. He was sentenced to concurrent terms of 15 months' imprisonment. A confiscation order was made against him under Proceeds of Crime Act (POCA) 2002 in the sum of nearly £22,000.[19]

The Fraud Act 2006 repealed the deception offences, replacing them with a single offence of fraud that may be committed in three ways, namely, by false representation (s 2),[20] by failing to disclose information (s 3) and by abuse of position (s 4). Each act or failure requires proof of dishonesty *and* an intention to make a gain or to cause loss, or to expose another person to the risk of loss.

Various "social security" offences exist, including (1) dishonestly making false statements, or producing false documents, or information;[21] (2) dishonestly failing to give prompt notification of a change of circumstances which he knows affects his entitlement to any benefit or other payment under relevant social security legislation;[22] (3) making a statement or representation (knowing it to be false) for the purposes of obtaining benefit or other payment under the relevant social security legislation;[23] (4) failing to give prompt notification of a change of circumstances which he knows affects his entitlement to any benefit or other payment under relevant social security legislation;[24] or (5) being knowingly concerned in the fraudulent evasion of any contribution which he/she or another person is liable to pay.[25] It is a "tax credit" offence to be knowingly concerned in any fraudulent activity undertaken with a view to obtaining a tax credit by the offender or by another person.[26] Various offences exist under the Forgery and Counterfeiting Act 1981 and under the Theft Act 1968 (notably theft of property). Many of the aforementioned offences can be committed inchoately (notably, criminal attempts,[27] statutory conspiracy,[28] conspiracy to defraud;[29] assisting or encouraging the commission of an offence,[30] e.g. a fraud).

In respect of "social security" payments, provision is made in the Social Security Administration Act 1992 for the exercise of discretion on the part of a relevant "authority" to impose a financial penalty as an alternative to prosecution.[31] As a matter of practice, every prosecuting authority has discretion not to prosecute any offence if it would not be in the public interest to do so. The 1992 Act also provides for the administrative recovery of certain benefits that have been overpaid.[32]

Property, including wages, obtained by criminal conduct, may be recoverable under an order of a court having criminal law jurisdiction (following conviction) or by a court exercising civil jurisdiction. Following conviction for an offence, a Magistrates' Court and a Crown Court have power to make one or more "ancillary orders"[33] against an offender, including a deprivation order (typically a forfeiture order),[34] the restitution of stolen goods[35] and/or an order for compensation.[36] A Magistrates' Court does not have power to make a "confiscation order" (i.e. under the Proceeds of Crime Act 2002) but it does have power to commit an offender to the Crown Court with a view to a confiscation order "being considered".[37] By contrast, it is open to the Crown Court to make confiscation orders as well as other ancillary orders (for example, a POCA "compliance order"[38] or a Serious Crime Prevention Order[39]).

Where confiscation proceedings under POCA 2002 have been initiated, public funds that were obtained by or "in connection with" an offence committed by a migrant ("criminal conduct"[40]) will constitute a "benefit"[41] in his or her hands. In cases where an offender has a "criminal lifestyle"[42] the confiscation provisions of POCA extend to any proceeds of crime (proved or assumed[43]) that he or she had obtained during the relevant statutory periods, regardless of whether or not the "criminal conduct" was the subject of a criminal charge before the court. The *full value* of the benefit is recoverable under a "confiscation order"[44] *unless* the offender proves (on a balance of probabilities) that his/her "available amount"[45] is worth less than the value of the benefit obtained. However, a confiscation order can be varied (without limit of time) to recover the balance of the value of the offender's "benefit" if further assets come to light (regardless of whether they were acquired before or after the making of the original order).[46]

Even in the absence of conviction, property that is held by a migrant, which can be shown[47] to represent the proceeds of his or her crime (i.e. "unlawful conduct"[48]) may constitute "recoverable property"[49] under one of the civil recovery regimes enacted under Part 5 of POCA 2002 (namely, chapters 2 and 3). The former ("Civil Recovery in The High Court or Court of Session") is a complex procedure that is deployed in cases where the value of the "recoverable property" is high. By contrast, chapter 3 ("Recovery of Cash in Summary Proceedings") is a simpler route by which "cash" may be seized and forfeited in summary proceedings. "Cash"[50] includes (but is not limited to) notes and coins in any currency, postal orders, cheques, travellers' cheques, bankers' drafts, bearer bonds and bearer shares.

However, applications to recover property by way of civil proceedings under POCA will fail unless the Crown is able to prove that the property was obtained by or in connection with a specific criminal offence, or an offence of an identifiable kind[51] (for example, social security fraud). In *Nuro v the Home Office*,[52] N failed to obtain leave to enter the UK under the Immigration Act 1971. He obtained £6500 as income for self-employed work as a handyman in respect of which (having acquired a national insurance number) he paid tax and national insurance contributions. N successfully appealed the decision of the Crown Court to uphold a Magistrates' Court order forfeiting the cash under chapter 3 to Part 5 of POCA 2002. N had worked when it was not a criminal offence for a migrant to obtain self-employed work once in the United Kingdom or to obtain a job there. It was not possible to establish a sufficient causal connection between N's illegal entry and the obtaining of his earnings, and it could not be inferred that he made false representations to anyone about his true immigration status. In order to find that N had perpetrated a fraud, the Crown Court would have had to have heard evidence about that, and it had not done so.

Despite the outcome in *Nuro* being fact-specific, the case was cited by the Government in a Written Answer given on 28 January 2016[53] to justify the insertion into the Immigration Act 1971[54] of s 24B that creates a summary offence of "illegal working"[55] to "address [*Nuro*] and provide a broader basis for cash seizure".[56] Under that provision, a person who is "subject to immigration control"[57] and who "knows or has reasonable cause to believe" that he/she is "disqualified"[58] from working by reason of his/her immigration status is liable to imprisonment for six months[59] and/or a fine. In addition, the prosecutor "must consider" whether to ask the Magistrates' Court to commit the offender to the Crown Court under s 70 POCA 2002 with a view to a confiscation order being considered.[60] Although the offence, in terms of its elements, is relatively straightforward to understand and to prove, the question of whether the offence is in the public interest, or likely to be counter-productive, is less easily answered. The Government intended that the offence should "serve as an important deterrent to illegal economic migrants"[61] and it sought "the removal of illegal workers from the UK"[62] subject to administrative and prosecutorial discretion to determine when it was, or was not, in the public interest to prosecute under s 24B of the 1971 Act. The contrary viewpoint is that it is better that vulnerable migrants, with an irregular immigration status, should work and earn money within the mainstream UK economic community rather than be placed at risk of exploitation by others.[63] That argument carried no weight with the government, remarking that "individuals with an irregular immigration status are already likely to be committing a criminal offence, regardless of whether they are working".[64] This is an over simplistic perspective. In *Nuro*,[65] the migrant's earnings were not tainted with illegality by reason of his irregular immigration status. In cases where a migrant has perpetrated a serious fraud[66] there are offences other than s 24B that are more suitable.

Even in cases where a migrant has committed the s 24B offence, and is liable to confiscation proceedings under POCA 2002, the question of whether or not such an order is proportionate will arise. Without the benefit of the s 24B offence, the earnings of a migrant might have been legitimately earned. In *R v Paulet* (mentioned above), the trial judge accepted that P had paid all the tax and national insurance that was due on his earnings, which had been "truly earned". The Court of Appeal[67] decided Paulet's appeal prior to the decision of the UK Supreme Court in *R v Waya*,[68] which held that a confiscation order (following conviction) should not be made to the extent that it would be disproportionate to do so, and thus a breach of Article 1 of Protocol 1 of the ECHR (A1P1). Following *Waya*, the issue of proportionality became a statutory requirement when the Crown Court is determining the "recoverable amount" under a confiscation order made under POCA 2002.[69] However, proportionality – as a legal concept – is protean (consider the commentary by the writer to *R v Box* [2018] Crim LR 578 at p. 581). In *R v Axworthy*,[70] Mr Justice Globe remarked that the effect of A1P1 is:

> that there must be a reasonable relationship of proportionality between the means employed by the state and the deprivation of property as a form of penalty and the legitimate aim which is sought to be realised by the deprivation. The legitimate aim and real essence of the Proceeds of Crime Act is to remove from criminals the pecuniary proceeds of their crime.

In the context of A1P1 and UK confiscation law, those remarks resonate with observations made by the UK Supreme Court in *R v Waya*,[71] the European Court of Human Rights in *Paulet v UK*[72] and, more recently, by the Court of Appeal (UK) in *R v Chahal*.[73]

However, the judicial pronouncements leave unclear the extent to which the "end" (recovering the proceeds of crime) justifies the "means" (making a confiscation order in accordance with POCA). They leave unclear the kind of cases in respect of which it would be disproportionate to make a confiscation order or to vary its value (other than where goods or money have been entirely restored to the loser[74]). What is clear from *R v Waya* is that the concept of proportionality does not vest a judge with a general discretion in the making of, or refusing to make, a confiscation order. All of this has implications for migrants whose earnings had been obtained illegally. The Supreme Court left open cases of disproportion that are analogous to that of goods or money entirely restored to the loser and which "will have to be resolved case by case as the need arises". The Court added that such a case:

> might include, for example, the defendant who, by deception, induces someone else to trade with him in a manner otherwise lawful, and who gives full value for goods or services obtained. He ought no doubt to be punished and, depending on the harm done and the culpability demonstrated, maybe severely, but whether a confiscation order is proportionate for any sum beyond profit made may need careful consideration.[75]

The above passage may provide some hope for a vulnerable migrant who (notwithstanding a conviction under s 24B(1A) 1971) might succeed in fending off the making of a confiscation order in respect of his or her earned income. Even in cases where the employer would not have employed the defendant had the latter's true immigration status been known, the employer has nonetheless received the "fruits" of the defendant's labour and skill – "fruits" that were likely to have been passed on, indirectly, to the employer's customers or clients.

In any event, the amount recoverable under a confiscation order following a conviction under s 24B is likely to be low. The offence is summary only (Magistrates' Court) and confiscation proceedings are rarely cost-effective. During debates in the House of Lords, the Government asserted that immigration offences had resulted in the confiscation of assets totalling £966,024 in 2014–2015. This statement was explained in a Written Answer[76] which disclosed that the sum related to 16 confiscation orders. Cases of "assisting unlawful immigration", "conspiracy to assist" and "assisting by sham marriage" accounted for confiscation orders totalling £350,000, £330,352.72 and £85,519.29, respectively. By contrast, cases of "fraud and money laundering" yielded a mere £2.00,[77] and "fraud by false representation" accounted for £1,020.32. The statistics do not reveal high value confiscation orders having being made in respect of migrants who had obtained income unlawfully. This is unsurprising (it is submitted) because migrants who earn money through the regular employment market (notwithstanding their irregular immigration status) are unlikely to be in a position to amass savings or assets of significant value. A confiscation order will only be made, if at all, to the value of the offender's existing wealth. The Written Answer does not disclose the amount of property actually realised in satisfaction of the confiscation orders made.

Migration and the reasons for it are complex issues that require skilful management and astute/humane policy-making. Migrants who aim to integrate with the host state and to be economically active (insofar as they are able to be so) may stray into offending rather than setting out to do so. The cost may be not only financial but also social. Problems associated with immigration are not readily resolved by the blunt instrument of the criminal law.

Notes

1 Version 3.0, published 1 February 2017.

2 *R. (on the application of Gureckis) v Secretary of State for the Home Department* [2017] EWHC 3298 (Admin) [2018] 4 WLR 9.

3 This was merely one of many legal representations made on behalf of the Home Department.

4 Mrs Justice Lang, judgment at [91].

5 Various news agencies provided this report (5 June 2014), including *The Times*, *The Daily Mail* and *Guardian*: www.theguardian.com/media/greenslade/2014/jun/05/the-big-issue-iain-duncan-smith.

6 23 May 2017. www.dailymail.co.uk/news/article-4535492/Judges-crack-EU-migrants-selling-Big-Issue.html.

7 *DV v Secretary of State for Work and Pensions* [2017] UKUT 1055 (AAC).

8 Such cases often turn on their facts: consider, for example, *Munteanu v Minister for Social Protection and others* [2017] IEHC 16.

9 See regs 14(1), 6(1) and 4(1) of the Immigration (European Economic Area) Regulations 2006. Note that SI 2006 No. 1003 was revoked and replaced by the Immigration (European Economic Area) Regulations 2016 (SI 2016 No. 1052; in force from 1 February 2017, subject to transitional provisions).

10 Reg. 6 of the Immigration (European Economic Area) Regulations 2006 (SI 2006 No. 1003; revoked by SI 2016 No. 1052 from 1 February 2017).

11 Article 49 of the *Treaty on the Functioning of the European Union* included the "right to take up and pursue activities as self-employed persons and to set up and manage undertakings, in particular companies and firms".

12 See *DV v SSWP* [2017] UKUT 0155 (AAC) citing (at [3]) *Jany v Staatssecretaris van Justitie* Case C-268/99, [2001] ECR I-8615.

13 See also *Revenue and Customs Commissioners v IT (CTC)* [2016] UKUT 252 (AAC) where IT's claim of "self-employment as a *Big Issue* seller was not 'effective and genuine' and was on such a small scale as to be regarded as purely marginal and ancillary" (at [25]).

14 [2001] UKUT 494.
15 [2011] UKUT 494 (at [11]).
16 15 January 2007.
17 These were the offences of obtaining "property", a "pecuniary advantage" and a "money transfer" by deception (ss 15, 15A, and 16 of the Theft Act 1968, respectively).
18 Conjoined with *Nelson* and *Pathak*, [2009] EWCA Crim 1573.
19 The latter order was held by a majority of the European Court of Human Rights to have been made in violation of article 1 of protocol 1 of the ECHR on the grounds that the question of the proportionality of the order had not been considered by the domestic courts.
20 A representation may be expressed or implied: s.2(4) Fraud Act 2006.
21 Section 111A(1), Social Security Administration Act 1992.
22 Section 111A(1A), Social Security Administration Act 1992.
23 Section 112(1), Social Security Administration Act 1992 (note that the word "dishonestly" does not appear in this provision and thus, it would seem, need not be proved: *Flintshire CC v Reynolds* [2006] EWHC 195 (Admin)).
24 Section 112(1A) of the Social Security Administration Act 1992 (note that the word "dishonestly" does not appear in this provision).
25 Section 114(1), Social Security Administration Act 1992.
26 Section 35(1), Tax Credit Act 2002, noting SI 2002 No.1727 (commencement provisions).
27 Criminal Attempts Act 1981.
28 Criminal Law Act 1977.
29 A common law offence.
30 Sections 44–46, Serious Crime Act 2007.
31 Section 115A, Social Security Administration Act 1992.
32 Section 71ZB, Social Security Administration Act 1992.
33 An expression used by the Sentencing Council in respect of the Definitive Guidelines it has published. For the Guidelines applicable in the Magistrates' Court, see www.sentencingcouncil.org.uk/wp-content/uploads/Sept-2015-MCSG-pdf1.pdf.
34 Powers of Criminal Courts (Sentencing) Act 200, s 143. However, this power applies in respect of property that was used "for the purpose of committing, or facilitating the commission of, any offence".
35 Powers of Criminal Courts (Sentencing) Act 2000, s 148. However, note that this is a limited power, namely, that it is exercisable in respect of property that has been "stolen" and which is held by a person (who need not be the offender).
36 Section 130, Powers of Criminal Courts (Sentencing) Act 2000.
37 Section 70, Proceeds of Crime Act 2002.
38 Section 13A, Proceeds of Crime Act 2002.
39 Pursuant to the Serious Crime Act 2007 in cases of an offender convicted of specified serious crimes, but includes fraud, counterfeiting and tax credit fraud.
40 See s 76(1), POCA [England and Wales], s 143(1) [Scot.] and s 224(1) [NI].
41 See s 76(4), POCA [E&W], s 143(4) [Scot.] and s 224(4) [NI].
42 Section 75 [E&W], s 142 [Scot.], s 223 [NI], POCA 2002.
43 POCA 2002 has enacted statutory assumptions that apply in a "criminal lifestyle" case in respect of property that was held, transferred to or expended by the offender during the specified statutory periods.
44 A "confiscation order" under POCA is *in personam* payable out of the offender's assets. It is not an order *in rem*.

45 See s 9, POCA [E&W], s 95 [Scot.] and s 159 [NI].
46 See s 22, POCA [E&W], s 107 [Scot], s 172 [NI], noting *In the matter of Peacock* [2012] UKSC 5.
47 On the balance of probabilities.
48 Section 241, POCA (Part 5, civil recovery).
49 Section 301(4), POCA 2002.
50 Section 289(6) POCA 2002.
51 *Director of the Assets Recovery Agency v Szepietowski* [2007] EWCA (Civ) 766, [2008] Lloyd's Rep FC 10, per Moore-Bick LJ at [106]–[107]; and see *National Crime Agency v Azam* [2014] EWHC 2722 (QB).
52 [2014] EWHC 462 (Admin).
53 www.parliament.uk/business/publications/written-questions-answers-statements/written-question/Lords/2016-01-20/HL5291 QUESTION: To ask Her Majesty's Government, further to the letter by Lord Bates to Lord Rosser on 8 January (DEP2016–0028) and the remarks by Lords Bates on 18 January (HL Deb, col 624), how they arrived at their assessment that in-country seizure could double with the use of the extended powers enabled by the new illegal working offence. ANSWER: The Government arrived at this assessment based on the impact of the court's judgement in the case of *Nuro* on the ability of Home Office Immigration Enforcement to use Proceeds of Crime Act (POCA) cash seizure powers which were conferred on immigration officers by section 24 of the UK Border Act 2007. The courts have held (*Nuro v Home Office* [2014]) that as it is not a criminal offence for an illegal immigrant who is not subject to immigration conditions to be self-employed in the UK, there is insufficient causation between the offence of illegal entry to the UK and obtaining the earnings to apply POCA powers. The creation of the offence of illegal working will address this judgement and provide a broader basis for cash seizure.
54 See s 34 of the Immigration Act 2016.
55 In force from 12 July 2016 (SI 2016 No. 603).
56 Written Answer, 28 January 2016: www.parliament.uk/business/publications/written-questions-answers-statements/written-question/Lords/2016-01-20/HL5291.
57 Section 24B(8), Immigration Act 1971.
58 Section 24B(1)(b), (2), Immigration Act 1971.
59 Subject to s 281(5), Criminal Justice Act 2003 coming into force, thereby raising the statutory maximum on summary jurisdiction to 51 weeks' imprisonment.
60 Section 24B(5), Immigration Act 1971 [E&W], s 24B(6) [Scot.] and s 24B(7) [NI].
61 *Hansard*, HL, 18 January 2016, per the Minister of State for the Home Office (Lord Bates), col. 625.
62 *Hansard*, HL, 18 January 2016, per the Minister of State for the Home Office (Lord Bates), col. 625.
63 See *Hansard*, HL, 22 December 2015, Second Reading.
64 *Hansard*, HL, 18 January 2016, per the Minister of State for the Home Office, col. 625.
65 [2014] EWHC 462 (Admin).
66 See, for example, *R v Turner* [2010] EWCA Crim 2897, where the offences committed by T were described by the Court as an "exercise of dishonest greed, by a woman with a sound financial base, making repeated gratuitous false declarations".

67 Conjoined with Nelson and Pathak, [2009] EWCA Crim 1573.
68 [2012] UKHL 51.
69 See the proviso to s 6(5) [E&W], s 92(6) [Scot.] and s 156(5) [NI], POCA 2002.
70 [2012] EWCA Crim 2889, at [9].
71 [2012] UKHL 51, at [20].
72 *Paulet v United Kingdom* (6219/08) Times, 19 May 2014 (ECHR); and see the commentary to that case, R. Fortson [2014] Crim L.R. 750.
73 [2015] EWCA Crim 816.
74 See *R v Waya*, at [30].
75 *R v Waya*, at [34].
76 Written Answer, HL 5290; 2 February 2016.
77 The figure of £2.00 probably reflects one or two cases where a court made a "nominal" order on the grounds that the offender's assets were insufficient to satisfy the confiscation order in full. Nominal orders are not indicative of the value of the property actually obtained by the offender.

11 Agricultural workers

Bethany Hastie

Overview

Formal labour migration programmes in the commercial agricultural sector have existed in several high-income countries for well over 50 years.[1] Over this time, the need for migrant labour in the agricultural sector has grown, and continues to do so.[2] In addition to countries with a lengthy history of such programmes, such as Canada and the United States,[3] new seasonal labour migration programmes are being created and implemented in countries such as New Zealand and Australia.[4] The comparatively high labour costs in agriculture is regularly put forth as a justification for maintaining low wages and intensive working conditions, which has, in turn, served as a justification for increasing and entrenched reliance on migrant labour in this industry.[5]

Agricultural labour migration programmes are often highly regulated by national governments, such as through bilateral agreements and formal government oversight.[6] These regulations govern recruitment and travel, conditions of work, wages, and living conditions for workers. Given the seasonal nature of agriculture, labour migration programmes most often operate on a circular basis, with workers migrating for a period of time each year, after which they must return home until the following season.[7]

This chapter discusses the costs attached to migrant agricultural labour in relation to each of the following topics: recruitment and travel; housing and transportation; wages and deductions; occupational health and safety; family separation; and remittances and development. Contrary to the "triple win" promise of labour migration as facilitating global development, this chapter will illustrate how agricultural labour migration programmes entrench a position of financial inequity for migrants, and exact significant costs, both monetary and otherwise, from agricultural workers.

Recruitment and travel

Unlike typical labour recruitment efforts, recruitment under seasonal agricultural worker programmes (SAWP) usually operates either on the basis of a contractor supply chain or directly through bilateral arrangements between a source and destination country.[8] Charging recruitment fees to a worker, or seeking reimbursement for recruitment fees from a worker, is often prohibited by law, though evidence suggests that such practices are common.[9] For example, it has been reported that migrant workers in Canada have been charged recruitment fees from $2,000 to $25,000.[10]

Agricultural labour migration programmes, as with most labour migration programmes, also often require fees to process visa applications for workers. Employers may be required to bear the cost of such fees; however, in some circumstances, workers are responsible for these costs. For example, in Canada, employers were historically required to pay visa application fees under SAWP; however, beginning in 2017, workers are responsible for paying such fees directly to the federal immigration department, currently set at $155.[11]

Depending on the programme and jurisdiction, agricultural workers may be responsible for bearing the cost of their travel to and from the country of work. For example, in most provinces in Canada, travel costs paid by an employer under the SAWP can be reclaimed through worker payroll deductions.[12] In contrast, workers participating in the US H-2A visa programme bear the cost of travel up-front, but must be reimbursed for the cost of travel to the place of work if they complete 50 per cent of the season and the cost of return travel if they complete the full season of work.[13]

Recruitment and transportation costs must also be understood in light of the dependence by workers on their employer for both current and future work. The cyclical nature of agricultural work often means that a worker is dependent on her employer for continued employment in future years. This has created a particular situation of (potential) exploitation, with the precarious employment and immigration status (current and future) of an agricultural worker largely in the hands of her employer.[14] This adds indirect costs, and also creates a situation where the financial costs migrant workers have already unfairly borne may add to the precariousness of their status.

Housing and daily transportation

Agricultural migrant worker programmes often include unique rules governing the provision of housing or accommodation. Under formalized agricultural labour migration programmes, employers are often required to provide housing for migrant workers.[15] Under some programmes, this housing must be provided at the employer's expense, while under others, an employer can deduct certain costs for housing from a worker's paycheque.[16] For example, in British Columbia, Canada, employers can deduct $5.36 per day from a worker's pay for accommodation, up to a maximum of $826 per season.[17] Housing is ostensibly subject to inspection to ensure adequate conditions; however, existing research documents inadequate housing conditions for migrant agricultural workers.[18]

For workers who live off-site, or far from the job site on a large property, daily transportation to and from their work site presents additional potential costs. While employers are required to provide transportation at no cost to workers in some jurisdictions, such as Canada, safety concerns inevitably arise. In addition, where this is not a requirement, workers may have to bear the additional costs – both financial and time – of daily transportation.

Wages and deductions

Migrant agricultural workers must be paid wages equal to those of domestic workers in many jurisdictions. However, differential wage structures and other substandard conditions for agricultural workers (regardless of citizenship status) are common in most destination countries.[19] For example, in British Columbia, Canada, agricultural workers can be paid by "piece-rate" for hand-harvesting work.[20] Differential wage structures are often justified as necessary to sustain local industry and remain competitive in an increasingly global marketplace. The result, however, is that remuneration for agricultural work is amongst the lowest of formally regulated job categories.[21] This has been posited as contributing to widespread job rejection by citizen workers in these countries, and thus to the dependence on migrant workers in this industry.[22]

In addition, workers may be required to pay into national contributory schemes, including employment insurance, pension programmes, and national health care schemes, as well as income tax, as a condition of their general employment in the country of work.[23] In such cases, these costs are often deducted from employees' paycheques. In other cases, migrant workers are not permitted to pay into such schemes, but as a result, cannot access those benefits.[24]

The low wages attached to migrant agricultural labour, coupled often with deductions for national social benefit schemes, and/or for housing and transportation (as discussed in the above section), means that migrant workers may receive very little net income during their employment. In addition, migrant agricultural workers may be practically excluded from obtaining the benefits of contributory schemes, despite paying into them for the duration of their employment.[25]

Occupational health and safety

Occupational health and safety is a heightened issue in agricultural work. The physically demanding nature of the work, coupled often with the presence of chemicals on site, presents acute job-related risks.[26] Countries that have mandatory occupational health and safety insurance often require employers to pay into such schemes for workers, including migrant agricultural workers.[27] In such cases, governing legislation may prevent such costs from being reimbursed by individual employers.

Despite the formal availability of occupational health and safety assistance and medical care, evidence suggests that these services may be practically inaccessible for workers.[28] Rather, given the ready supply of additional labourers, workers who experience injury or illness on the job may simply be terminated and returned to their countries of origin, where they will have to bear the cost of medical treatment independently.[29]

Family separation

The seasonal nature and regulatory structure of agricultural labour migration programmes generally do not permit workers' families to travel with them. In addition, some programmes, like Canada's SAWP, selectively recruit participants who have a family or dependants to support at home, as these participants are seen as more reliable.[30] Migrant agricultural workers not only endure a substantial length of time away from their families each year, they often also are the primary, or sole, financial support for their families back home. In addition to the monetary costs associated with circular agricultural migration, as detailed in the previous sections, the separation of family has been documented as a broader cost and negative consequence of low-wage labour migration, generally, in the globalized marketplace.[31]

Remittances and development

Labour migration programmes, including seasonal agricultural programmes, are predicated on a "triple win" scenario: host countries benefit from the "just in time" labour needed to fill domestic shortages; origin countries benefit from the increase in remittances, which supports domestic economic growth; and individual workers benefit from the income-earning opportunity they may not otherwise have in their origin country.[32]

Remittances play an important role in this equation. For example, under Canada's SAWP, remittances to Mexico were reported at $174.1 million CAD in 2012, with the average remittance total per worker being just under $10,000 in that same year.[33] Remittances are most often used by family members "for expenses such as buying land and homes; household appliances and repairs; debt payments; feeding, clothing and educating children; and medical expenses".[34]

Despite the impact of remittances on the daily lives of workers and their families, evidence increasingly suggests that, rather than contribute to economic development in a sustainable manner, low-wage labour migration programmes create a relationship of long-term economic dependence and facilitate exploitation of migrant workers.[35]

A recent report for the International Labour Organization synthesized data on agricultural labour migration programmes in four countries: Canada, the United States, Spain, and New Zealand/Australia.[36] Positive impacts from remittances were hypothesized to likely be "intergenerational", affecting the children and subsequent generations of current migrant workers.[37] However, under the comparatively new New Zealand programme, the report states that workers tended to return home with savings and better English.[38] Similarly, in respect of Canada, remittances are stated to have improved housing conditions, as well as children's health and education, in origin countries.[39]

Conclusion

Overall, while seasonal agricultural labour migration programmes may be seen as a stable and positive contribution to the global marketplace, and to international labour migration governance, in reality, these programmes come at a significant cost for migrant workers. Although seasonal agricultural work provides migrant workers with a long-term, stable job opportunity, the wages and working conditions, in practice, minimize the benefits of that opportunity. Workers earn low wages compared with the average wages for citizen workers in a variety of occupations, but often face greater deductions, not only for national social benefit schemes, but also, uniquely compared to citizen workers, for housing and transportation. Agricultural workers are also at a heightened risk of injury or illness on the job, with an equally high risk that such a consequence will cause job loss, and that the worker will have to pay the costs of medical treatment independently once returned to their origin country.

Coupled with the many direct financial costs detailed in this chapter, migrant agricultural workers may also spend decades regularly living apart from their families, contributing to deeper costs associated with family separation. Finally, the positive benefits related to remittances and development put forth in relation to agricultural labour migration programmes, like with all low-wage labour migration, are not being adequately realized by workers in their origin countries.

Notes

1 See Stephen Castles, "Back to the Future? Can Europe Meet its Labour Needs through Temporary Migration?", IMI Working Paper No 1 (2006), online: www.imi.ox.ac.uk/publications/wp-01-06; Cindy Hahamovitch, "Creating Perfect Immigrants: Guestworkers of the Word in Historical Perspective", *Labor History* 44, no. 1 (2003): 69.

2 See ILO, *International Labour Migration: A Rights-Based Approach* (Geneva: ILO, 2010); Catherine Dauvergne and Sarah Marsden, "Beyond Numbers Versus Rights: Shifting the Parameters of Debate on Temporary Labour Migration", *Journal of International Migration & Integration* 15 (2014): 525; Martin Ruhs and Philip Martin, "Numbers vs. Rights: Trade-Offs and Guest Worker Programs", *International Migration Review* 42, no. 1 (2008): 249.

3 See, e.g., Kerry Preibisch and Jenna L. Hennebry, "Buy Local, Hire Global: Temporary Migration in Canadian Agriculture", in *Legislated Inequality: Temporary Labour Migration in Canada*, Patti Tamara Lenard and Christine Straehle, eds. (Montreal: McGill-Queen's University Press, 2012); Kitty Calavita, *Inside the State: The Bracero Program, Immigration, and the I.N.S.* (New York: Routledge, 1992). The *Immigration and Nationality Act 1952* in the United States introduced a general H-2 work visa programme, which was subdivided by the *Immigration Control and Reform Act of 1986*, creating the current H-2A and H-2B model.

4 See Christine Brickenstein, "Impact Assessment of Seasonal Labor Migration in Australia and New Zealand: A Win–Win Situation?", *Asian and Pacific Migration Journal* 24, no. 1 (2015): 107; John Gibson and David McKenzie, "Development through Seasonal Worker Programs: The Case of New Zealand's RSE Program", in *International Handbook on Migration and Economic Development*, Robert E. B. Lucas, ed. (Northampton, MA: Edward Elgar Publishing, 2014).

5 See ILO, *Migrant Workers in Commercial Agriculture* (Geneva: ILO, 2016); Jenna L. Hennebry and Kerry Preibisch, "A Model for Managed Migration? Re-Examining Best Practices in Canada's Seasonal Agricultural Worker Program", *International Migration*, 50 (2010): 19.

6 Christiane Kuptsch, "Inequalities and the Impact of Labour Market Institutions on Migrant Workers", in *Labour Markets, Institutions and Inequality: Building Just Societies in the 21st Century*, Janine Berg, ed. (Northampton, MA: Edward Elgar Publishing, 2015) at 353–354. See also ILO, *Migrant Workers*; Patti Tamara Lenard and Christine Straehle, "Introduction", in *Legislated Inequality: Temporary Labour Migration in Canada*, Patti Tamara Lenard and Christine Straehle, eds. (Montreal: McGill-Queen's University Press, 2012).

7 For example, under Canada's SAWP, workers may remain in Canada for up to eight months per year, and may be individually named by an employer to return the following season. Under the US H-2A programme, workers can remain for up to ten months.

8 ILO, *Migrant Workers*, 13.

9 See Fay Faraday, *Profiting from the Precarious: How Recruitment Practices Exploit Migrant Workers* (Toronto, ON: Metcalfe Foundation, 2014); House of Commons, Standing Committee on Citizenship and Immigration, "Temporary Foreign Workers and Non-Status Workers" (May 2009) (Chair: David Tilson, MP); UNODC, *The Role of Recruitment Fees and Abusive and Fraudulent Recruitment Practices of Recruitment Agencies in Trafficking in Persons* (Vienna: UNODC, 2015); Natalia Ollus, Anniina Jokinen, and Matti Joutsen, eds., *Exploitation of Migrant Workers in Finland, Sweden, Estonia and Lithuania: Uncovering the Links Between Recruitment, Irregular Employment Practices and Labour Trafficking* (Helsinki: European Institute for Crime Prevention and Control, 2013).

10 House of Commons, 30.

11 See ESDC, "Hire a Temporary Worker Through the Seasonal Agricultural Worker Program", online: www.canada.ca/en/employment-social-development/services/foreign-workers/agricultural/seasonal-agricultural.html; CIC, "Fee List", online: www.cic.gc.ca/english/information/fees/fees.asp. The US H-2A programme is "unique" in that it requires employers to bear all costs for workers, including visa application and processing: ILO, *Migrant Workers*, 15.

12 Except British Columbia. ESDC, "Hire a Temporary Worker". Similar structures for cost sharing of travel exist in New Zealand, Australia, and Spain: ILO, *Migrant Workers*, 13.

13 USDOL, "Fact Sheet #26: Section H-2A of the Immigration and Nationality Act (INA)", online: www.dol.gov/whd/regs/compliance/whdfs26.pdf.

14 See, e.g., Hennebry and Preibisch, "A Model for Managed Migration?"; Jenna Hennebry, "Permanently Temporary? Agricultural Migrant Workers and Their Integration in Canada", *IRPP* No. 26 (2012); Kerry Preibisch, "Pick-Your-Own Labour: Migrant Workers and Flexibility in Canadian Agriculture", *International Migration Review* 44, no. 2 (2010): 404; Preibisch and Hennebry, "Buy Local, Hire Global".

15 ILO, *Migrant Workers*, 10.

16 See "Agreement for the Employment in Canada of Seasonal Agricultural Workers from Mexico – 2017", online: www.canada.ca/content/dam/canada/employment-social-development/migration/documents/assets/portfolio/docs/en/foreign_workers/hire/seasonal_agricultural/documents/sawpmc2017.pdf. Under the H-2A visa programme in the US, employers must provide free housing or accommodation to workers (USDOL).

17 Ibid.

18 Hennebry, "Permanently Temporary?", 10. See also Q. M. Vallejos, S. A. Quandt, J. G. Grzywacz, S. Isom, H. Chen, L, Galván, L. Whalley, A. B. Chatterjee, and T. A. Arcury, "Migrant Farmworkers' Housing Conditions Across an Agricultural Season in North Carolina", *American Journal of Industrial Medicine* 54 (2011): 533.

19 Kuptsch, "Inequalities", 348–349. See also Janet McLaughlin, "Classifying the 'Ideal Migrant Worker': Mexican and Jamaican Transnational Farmworkers in Canada", *Focaal – Journal of Global and Historical Anthropology* 57 (2010): 79; Fay Faraday, *Made in Canada How the Law Constructs Migrant Workers' Insecurity* (Toronto, ON: Metcalf Foundation, 2012) at n232.

20 See: www2.gov.bc.ca/gov/content/employment-business/employment-standards-advice/employment-standards/factsheets/farm-workers.

21 ILO, *Migrant Workers*.
22 Ibid.
23 Brickenstein, "Impact Assessment", 114–115; R. Holzmann and Y. Pouget, "Social Protection for Temporary Migrant Workers: Conceptual Framework, Country Inventory, Assessment and Guidance. A Study Prepared for the Global Forum of Migration and Development", World Bank and Marseille Center for Mediterranean Integration, Marseille, France, 27 October 2010, at 31, 62; W. Van Ginneken, "Social Protection for Migrant Workers: National and International Policy Challenges", *European Journal of Social Security* 15, no. 2 (2013): 209 at 213, 218; ILO, *Migrant Workers*.
24 Brickenstein, "Impact Assessment", 114–116.
25 Jenna Hennebry, Janet McLaughlin, and Kerry Preibisch, "Out of the Loop: (In)access to Health Care for Migrant Workers in Canada", *International Migration and Integration* 17 (2016): 521.
26 Brickenstein, "Impact Assessment", 115; ILO, *Migrant Workers*, 11; K. Mobed, E. B. Gold, and M. B. Schenker. "Occupational Health Problems Among Migrant and Seasonal Farm Workers", *Western Journal of Medicine* 157, no. 3 (1992): 367.
27 E.g., ESDC, "Hire a Temporary Worker"; USDOL, "Fact Sheet #26".
28 Hennebry, McLaughlin, and Preibisch, "Out of the Loop".
29 For example, under Canada's SAWP, a worker may be "repatriated" to their country of origin within 24–48 hours of termination, and without a substantive review of the reasons for termination or opportunity to appeal: Faraday, "Made in Canada", 93.
30 Don Wells, André Lyn, Janet McLaughlin, and Aaraón Díaz Mendiburo, "Sustaining Precarious Transnational Families: The Significance of Remittances from Canada's Seasonal Agricultural Workers Program", *Just Labour* 22 (2014): 144.
31 Ibid.
32 Brickenstein, "Impact Assessment"; ILO, *Migrant Workers*; S. Ramasamy, V. Krishnan, R. Bedford, and C. Bedford, "The Recognised Seasonal Employer Policy: Seeking the Elusive Triple Wins for Development Through International Migration", *Pacific Economic Bulletin* 23 (2008): 171; Ruhs and Martin, "Numbers vs. Rights"; Kuptsch, "Inequalities", 353–354.
33 Wells *et al.*, "Sustaining Precarious Transnational Families", 145.
34 Ibid., 146.
35 Brickenstein, "Impact Assessment"; ILO, *Migrant Workers*.
36 ILO, *Migrant Workers*.
37 Ibid., 15.
38 Ibid., 14.
39 Ibid., 14.

12 The migrant tax – how children and young people pay to exercise mobility rights

Jacqueline Bhabha

We will protect the human rights and fundamental freedoms of all refugee and migrant children, regardless of their status, and giving primary consideration at all times to the best interests of the child.

(High level meeting of the UN General Assembly on addressing large movements of refugees and migrants, 19 September 2016.[1] [underline added])

Over 50 per cent of global refugees are children and 13 per cent of global migrants are children. Neither of these are dramatic recent developments – they are patterns that have been in place for years. Nevertheless, concerns about the human rights violations to which children on the move are subject, both as they move across borders and as refugees and immigrants after their arrival, have only recently been widely expressed. Also recent is the high-level attention to lacunae in child migration policy, including in the measures used to receive, house and make decisions about children. Efforts are now underway to ensure that the ambitious promises articulated in the September 2016 UN New York Declaration on large movements of refugees and migrants, cited above, are translated into workable and sustainable policies whose impact can be measured and evaluated.[2]

The belated surge of concern is welcome. It has long been known that child migrants and refugees experience egregious detriments because of their triple status – as children, non-citizens, distress migrants. These detriments start prior to departure as a result of the risks of conflict or the trauma of natural disaster and endure as lifelong impacts on both economic and non-economic aspects of child migrants' futures.[3] Children of school age during World War II in and from Germany displayed poorer health outcomes and self-reported health satisfaction even in late adulthood.[4] UNICEF reports that adolescent boys from Sub-Saharan Africa crossing the Central Mediterranean route (from Libya to Southern Italy), despite a secondary education and the advantage of travelling in a group, face a 73 per cent risk of being exploited.[5] For children without education, the risk of exploitation rises to 90 per cent.[6] According to Amnesty International, Syrian child refugees en route through Turkey to Europe have been denied health care and social protection, with some unaccompanied children forcibly returned to Syria.[7] Instances of Somali child refugees suffering from malnutrition while on the move to Ethiopia have been documented.[8] A 2017 report in *The Independent* noted that sexual violence against young girls and women, some as young as 13, was so common on the migration route through North Africa that people smugglers had begun injecting refugees with contraceptives in anticipation that they would be raped.[9] The negative impacts of circumstances precipitating distress migration are exacerbated where transit and receiving societies thus fail to adequately implement their child protection and broader human rights obligations to care for children within their jurisdictions.

These failures are not accidental but systemic, a product of pervasive discrimination against non-citizen children and the result of political and social structures driven primarily by migration control imperatives rather than the uniform obligations of protection and care that states have towards all children in their territory.

Ironically, children – despite their universally recognized claim to state protection[10] – have less access to legal, safe or regular migration options as a group than adults do and are thus at greater risk of abuse, violence and exploitation. Their exercise of mobility is fraught with related dangers. This is particularly the case for adolescents, whether their migration occurs in the global South or in the global North. A report by Save the Children entitled "Protecting Syrian Children en route to Europe" documented the presence of "mental health risks" and the need for psychosocial supports for children on the move, noting particularly that facilities and protections for adolescents were sorely lacking.[11] Even more basic access to primary health care services is severely inadequate. An example is the recent finding that 91 per cent of refugee children in Greece did not have the recommended vaccinations.[12]

The failures to extend to child migrants basic protections accorded to citizen children do not only occur while children are on the move. Many studies document the failure of host countries to accord to migrant, refugee or immigrant children fundamental human rights protections available to citizen children, either because of inherently discriminatory access procedures or as a result of failures to proactively reach out to a population known to be particularly in need of targeted services.

A case in point is access to education, whether to early childhood education – known to be a key trigger of future integration and successful engagement in the host society – or to the public school system. Though education is one of the most keenly sought after benefits aspired to by children on the move, whether they are refugees or have migrated for other reasons, access to education is elusive and often unreasonably difficult. Refugee children are five times more likely to be out of school than other children, with only 50 per cent and 25 per cent enrolled in primary and secondary school respectively.[13] This is a sorry state of affairs that violates international law obligations set out in the UN Convention on the Status of Refugees[14] and the UN Convention on the Rights of the Child.[15]

Not only does this violation of the right to education deprive children of a critical element for promoting a sense of normalcy and reducing stress, it also affects refugee children's future employment and therefore economic prospects, exacerbating risks of child labour and child marriage, additional serious human rights detriments.[16] Even in countries where considerable efforts and investment in services have been made, children on the move can face considerable structural, administrative and legal barriers that undermine educational equity.[17] For migrant children, the situation may also be grave. Only 10 out of 28 EU Member States recognize the right of undocumented children to enter the school system, and five explicitly exclude them from free schooling. Even when legal barriers are not decisive, migrant children face pervasive stigma and discrimination.[18] Children who are undocumented or living in families with undocumented members also have to face the crippling fear of official scrutiny of their status and of deportation or other negative repercussions for themselves or their families.[19]

"Migrant premium" is not exactly the right framework for exploring the detriments to rights and protection that affect children as a result of migration. That framing implies some quid pro quo, some ensuing benefit or consideration, whether economic, social or cultural, flowing to the child from the hardships associated with migrant status, an advantage offset by the levy of a premium. But most children do not have enhanced income-generating potential following their migration, as is the case for adults. Nor is it appropriate to assume that they enjoy higher overall benefits – better schooling, broader health coverage, a safer social environment, as is typically claimed for adults. Even the cultural fruits of migration vary – depending on the age of arrival and the legal status of the child and his or her family.[20]

For children, the opportunities and benefits afforded by migration may be elusive, outweighed by the detriments – the trauma of separation from home, the hardships associated with the journey, the challenges of integration – bullying, sexual exploitation, absence of family or other carers, even homelessness. At the same time, reputational and financial costs often preclude return to the status quo ante, namely retracing one's steps home.

Far more than adults, child migrants, particularly those travelling alone, lack access to safe and legal avenues for exercising their mobility. To be sure, children have access to a legal and regular migration status when they accompany or travel to join parents or other carers legitimately exercising mobility rights – parents travelling for work, to study, to invest, to seek asylum or to join sponsoring relatives, for example. They also have such access when they come from economically prosperous or socially privileged families – families that can pay high foreign student fees, and facilitate advantageous adolescent experiences and training opportunities. But otherwise as independent migrants, as adolescents seeking educational opportunities or internships or skill training or jobs, their chances of securing a legal migration status are minimal – close to nil if they are not backed by these adult links or networks. Yet these are the reasons most young people, with the exception of those seeking asylum or resettlement as refugees, feel a strong "migration instinct" and wish to exercise their mobility.[21] Theirs is a distress migration in response to aspirations for a better future, and to intolerable home circumstances (child abuse, destitution following decades of conflict and family destruction, as in Afghanistan, Somalia, Sudan and the DRC, or a sense of hopelessness and imminent danger at home, as in the murderous cities of the Central American Northern Triangle).

Because one cannot take for granted the implicit improvements in the baseline living circumstances for children following migration compared to their situation before, improvements which set the context for the payment of a premium (however excessive) it makes more sense, when evaluating the costs and benefits of migration for children, to speak of migrant tax rather than migrant premium.

The de facto "taxes" on security and wellbeing imposed on children simply because of their non-citizen status are widespread. A study focusing on the experiences of child refugees from South Sudan residing in Ugandan refugee settlements noted lack of access to health care as a significant concern.[22] Zimbabwean child refugees struggle to access health care services because of language barriers and stigmatization by health care workers in South Africa.[23] These serious, mobility related, detriments also affect child migrants in the global North. A 2016 report by Human Rights Watch noted that unaccompanied refugee children in Sweden, primarily arriving from Syria but also from Iraq and Eritrea, had been denied access to health care services, including post-rape gynaecological care, in large part because of the insensitive or discriminatory attitudes of health care workers.[24]

The National Child Traumatic Stress Network (NCTSN) has also documented the phenomenon of "acculturative stress" as a potential source of mental health difficulties for child refugees in destination settings.[25] Discrimination and social isolation may also exacerbate this challenge.[26]

Taking note of previous child protection failures in the implementation of reception and integration policies for child migrants and refugees, some states have made laudable attempts to address protection deficits and institute non-discriminatory policies. Two contrasting examples are instructive – one a migrant-specific policy specifically geared to addressing vulnerable children's protection needs, the other a child-specific approach geared to removing the migrant tax inappropriately levied on non-citizen children by including all minors within domestic child protection schemes. The first example is the US visa accorded to particularly vulnerable children who qualify for the Special Immigrant Juvenile Status, or SIJS. This form of "immigration relief" available only to non-citizen children who have been abused, abandoned or neglected is "the most reliable conduit to a regular and permanent immigration status in the US".[27] Conceived as an answer to the problems arising from the presence of undocumented children in the domestic foster care or juvenile justice systems, the SIJS visa is granted where a consideration of the child's best interests reveals that he or she should not be returned to the country of origin, but rather should be cared for in the US. Thanks to this remedy, thousands of vulnerable non-citizen children have thus been afforded substantial care and protection, rather than the inferior treatment many of their peers elsewhere are subjected to.

The second is the non-discriminatory approach developed by the Italian authorities to ensure that domestic child protection services and responsibilities are as applicable and accessible to migrant and refugee children as they are to citizen children. Italy is one of the countries where prioritization of the best interests of all children, including non-citizen children, is most established. In May 2017, a new law on "Protection Measures for Unaccompanied Minors" was passed, by virtue of which unaccompanied minors are entitled to the same protections as Italian children, within the mainstream child welfare system. Though budget shortfalls and programming failures in response to large recent migrant arrival numbers have undermined the efficacy of this new measure, it stands as an excellent example of how to remove the common practice of taxing children for exercising mobility.

Both these precedents provide instructive pointers for the future. They can and should feed into the ongoing process of discussion and deliberation taking place in response to the UN's launch of the two Global Compacts and the generative policy debates building up to the 2018 high level discussion on large scale movements of people (including children) to be held by the UN. The opportunities afforded by an unprecedented global focus on migration and refugee management, with the UN set to launch two new global compacts in September 2018, generate responsibilities for advancing just, workable and sustainable solutions to some of the key current rights deficits. The confluence of human rights, migration management and development focused goals set out in recent UN programmes, most notably in the Sustainable Development Goals and in the New York Declaration, provides a framework for the formulation of such solutions. By taking seriously the consensual aspirations quoted at the outset and already articulated in the Declaration and by operationalizing relevant aspects of the SDGs, it is possible to craft a set of compelling and practical recommendations relevant to the circumstances of child migrants and refugees.[28]

Notes

1 Declaration for the 19 September high level meeting of the UN General Assembly on addressing large movements of refugees and migrant, Section 1.11.

2 Jacqueline Bhabha and Mike Dottridge (24 June 2017) *Child Rights in the Global Compacts: Recommendations for protecting, promoting and implementing the human rights of children on the move in the proposed Global Compacts*.

3 For details of the safety and psychological risks facing children from forced displacement and relocation, a major element of global child migration, see T. Tamashiro (2010) *Impact of Conflict on Children's Health and Disability*. http://unesdoc.unesco.org/images/0019/001907/190712e.pdf.

4 M. Akbulut-Yuksel (2009) "Children of war: The long-run effects of large-scale physical destruction and warfare on children", IZA Discussion Paper 4407.

5 UNICEF and IOM (September 2017) *Harrowing Journeys: Children and youth on the move across the Mediterranean*. www.unicef.org/publications/index_100621.html.

6 Ibid.

7 Amnesty International (2016) "Turkey: Illegal mass returns of Syrian refugees expose fatal flaws in EU-Turkey deal". www.amnesty.org/en/press-releases/2016/04/turkey-illegal-mass-returns-of-syrian-refugees-expose-fatal-flaws-in-eu-turkey-deal/.

8 B. S. Porras (2011) "Ethiopia: Malnourished Somali refugees seek shelter in camps". http://allafrica.com/stories/201112192263.html.

9 W. Worley (2017) "People smugglers 'inject refugee children with contraceptive' due to high chance they will be raped". www.independent.co.uk/news/world/africa/refugee-crisis-rape-sexual-violence-pregnancy-contraception-injected-progesterone-a7575936.html.

10 Art. 3, UN Convention on the Rights of the Child 1989.

11 Save the Children (2017) "Protecting Syrian children en route to Europe". https://resourcecentre.savethechildren.net/node/12177/pdf/protecting_syrian_children_en_route_to_europe_feb_2017.pdf.

12 I. D. Pavlopoulou, M. Tanaka, S. Dikalioti, E. Samoli, P. Nisianakis, O. D. Boleti and K. Tsoumakas (2017) "Clinical and laboratory evaluation of new immigrant and refugee children arriving in Greece". *BMC Pediatrics*, 17, 132.

13 UNICEF (September 2017) *Education Uprooted.* www.refworld.org/docid/59c1259a4.html.

14 Art. 22, UN Convention on the Status of Refugees, 1951.

15 Art. 28, UN Convention on the Rights of the Child, 1989.

16 No Lost Generation (April 2017) "Preparing for the future of children and youth in Syria and the region through education: London one year on", Brussels Conference Education Report, NLG, p. 5.

17 United Nations Children's Fund (September 2016) "Uprooted: The growing crisis for refugee and migrant children", UNICEF, New York, p. 39.

18 P. Bourgonje (2010) "Education for refugee and asylum seeking children in OECD countries: Case studies from Australia, Spain, Sweden and the United Kingdom". https://download.ei-ie.org/Docs/WebDepot/EIResearch_Paloma_Eng_final_med.pdf.

19 UNICEF (September 2017) *Education Uprooted.* www.refworld.org/docid/59c1259a4.html.

20 C. Suárez-Orozco and M. Suárez-Orozco (2001) *Children of Immigration* (Cambridge, MA: Harvard University Press).

21 Gonzalo Sánchez-Teran (forthcoming 2018) "The global forced migration crisis and the education of children", in Marcelo Suárez Orozco, ed., *Disrupted Lives: The forceful displacement of refugee children and new directions for research* (Los Angeles, CA: University of California Press).

22 B. Paardekooper, J. T. V. M de Jong and J. M. A. Hermanns (1999) "The psychological impact of war and the refugee situation on South Sudanese children in refugee camps in Northern Uganda: An exploratory study". *Journal of Child Psychology and Psychiatry*, 40, 529–36.

23 L. Meda (2017) *Refugee Learner Experiences: A case study of Zimbabwean refugee children* (Hamburg: Anchor Academic Publishing).

24 Human Rights Watch (2016) "Seeking refuge: Unaccompanied children in Sweden". www.hrw.org/sites/default/files/report_pdf/sweden0616web_1.pdf.

25 National Child Traumatic Stress Network (2005) "Mental health interventions for refugee children in resettlement". www.nctsn.org/sites/default/files/resources//mental_health_interventions_refugee_children_resettlement.pdf.

26 Ibid.

27 Veronica Thronson (forthcoming 2018) "The impact of Special Immigrant Juvenile Status on access to protection of unaccompanied child migrants to the United States", in Jacqueline Bhabha, Jyothi Kanics and Daniel Senovilla Hernandez, eds, *Research Handbook on Child Migration* (Cheltenham: Edward Elgar Publishing).

28 For an example, see Jacqueline Bhabha and Mike Dottridge (24 June 2017) *Child Rights in the Global Compacts: Recommendations for protecting, promoting and implementing the human rights of children on the move in the proposed Global Compacts.*

13 Migrant remittances in the face of securitization

Anthony Amicelle

> By 2030, reduce to less than 3 per cent the transaction costs of migrant remittances and eliminate remittance corridors with costs higher than 5 per cent.[1]

Introduction

Remittances refer to person-to-person transfers of relatively small amounts of money from one country to another. In this regard, migrant workers rely on remittance services on a large scale to send a portion of their earnings to their relatives. According to the World Bank, 232 million migrants were involved in remittance transactions in 2016 for a total of $575 billion, including $429 billion to developing countries.[2] It is more than three times the official development assistance and more than foreign direct investments to almost every single developing country.[3] "Taken together – senders and their families back home – 1 billion people are directly involved with remittances: one out of seven people in the world."[4] These remittances are widely used by low-skilled migrant workers and their families in the country of origin to cover basic needs such as food and housing whilst contributing to support education and health care, as well as for savings and small investments. Annual remittance flows equal more than $100 million for 100 countries on the receiving end, representing over 3 per cent of GDP for 71 countries and over 20 per cent of GDP for 9 countries in Africa, Asia and the Middle East.[5] Half of these flows come from ten major remittance sending countries, six out of ten from the G8 countries: France, Germany, Italy, Russia, the United Kingdom and the United States.

In this context, it is certainly no coincidence that G8 heads of government and states made undertakings on the cost of remittance services. Their "5x5 objective" – the objective of reducing the global average cost of sending $200 in remittances by 5 per cent in 5 years – was adopted at the 2009 G8 summit in Italy and then endorsed by the G20 countries in

2011. To a certain extent, this commitment paved the way to the objective called for in SDG 10.C of the UN's 2030 agenda for sustainable development. Achieving the "5x5 objective" would save $16 billion per year for the migrants and their families according to the World Bank, while reaching the UN SDG 10.C would save $20 billion per year according to the Global Migration Group.[6] However, the 5 per cent objective is still far from being achieved over five years after the G8/G20 commitment, and the remaining progress to meet the 3 per cent UN SDG is substantial.

"While remittances can be a lifeline for families and communities of international migrant workers in their countries of origin, the high cost of transferring money continues to reduce such benefits."[7] Remittance fees are far above official targets to the extent that the global average cost of sending $200 is over 7.2 per cent in 2017 by contrast to about 9.5 per cent in 2009.[8] Furthermore, there is an estimated 61 per cent of remittance corridors with costs higher than 5 per cent.[9] Transfer costs vary from one country, region and continent to another and depending on the type of remittance service providers. On the one hand, sending remittances to and within the African continent is proportionately the most expensive, especially to the Sub-Saharan Africa region (over 9 per cent) and from South Africa to surrounding countries (over 16 per cent).[10] The highest costs are very often located in the poorest and rural areas while an estimated 40 per cent of total remittance flows goes to these areas.[11] With regards to the top ten remittance sending countries, the six out of ten from the G8 remain all above the targets (France – over 6.5 per cent; Germany – over 7.5 per cent; Italy – about 6 per cent; the United Kingdom – about 7 per cent; the United States – about 5.7 per cent) except Russia – about 2.1 per cent. On the other hand, the global average cost of sending remittances also differs between the four main types of formal remittance service providers, from banks (11 per cent) to post offices (over 6.5 per cent), money transfer operators as the dominant type of providers in almost every sending country, starting with Western Union, MoneyGram and Ria (about 6.1 per cent), and mobile operators (about 3.1 per cent).[12]

"With over $400 billion officially recorded flows to developing countries remittances are a critical source of national and families' income. However, high transaction costs and other inefficiencies in the process often adversely impact migrant workers and their families."[13] What are the reasons for these remaining high transaction costs and other inefficiencies? Beyond fluctuations of the foreign exchange market and cyclical financial and economic crisis, a list of explanations is regularly provided by international organizations such as the UN and the World Bank: (1) lack of financial infrastructure in some sending and receiving countries; (2) low level of competition and lack of transparency in the markets; (3) regulatory obstacles; (4) lack of access to the banking services by remittance senders and receivers, including money transfer operators; and (5) difficulties for migrants to obtain and provide requested identification documents to access financial services.[14] Interestingly enough, most of these explanations – if not all – can be connected, to varying degrees, with the securitization of migrant remittances. This securitization entails that remittance activities are partly rendered and governed as national and international security problems in the name of anti-money laundering and counter-terrorism. The most recent and illustrative adverse effect of such a securitization certainly relates to the de-risking phenomenon and its detrimental consequences on the remittance sector.

According to the international policy-making body on money laundering and terrorist financing (Financial Action Task Force – FATF), de-risking refers to the phenomenon of financial institutions terminating or restricting business relationships with clients or categories of clients to avoid, rather than manage, risk.[15] Since 2015, various studies have shown how banks' de-risking practices represent a critical issue for the provision of remittance services.[16]

> Complaining that remittance transactions are prone to the risk of money laundering and other financial crimes, banks have been closing the correspondent banking accounts of many money-transfer operators (MTOs). [...] The [World Bank] survey results confirmed that MTO account closures by banks was widespread, with obvious adverse impact on remittance costs and access to remittance services in rural and remote regions.[17]

De-risking behaviour seems to be one of the most prominent consequences of years of securitization of migrant remittances.

Drawing on document analysis and former qualitative fieldworks in the UK and Canada, the chapter aims to question this securitization process and its adverse effects on migrants from the post-9/11 focus on informal remittance systems to the ongoing challenges encountered by formal remittance services and their customers.

Suspicion and exclusion from informal to formal remittance services

The securitization of informal remittance services

According to the FATF:

> [Y]ears after September 11th and the adoption of Special Recommendation VI on Alternative Remittance Systems, two often competing

> and conflicting views on hawala still stand. Many countries and communities, as well as the development community, view them as essential providers of financial services to the unbanked in countries with limited financial access. In significant numbers of jurisdictions and sometimes in the same jurisdiction, law enforcement views them as one of the leading channels for terrorist financing and money laundering.[18]

Although the proportion of informal remittance flows – often through unlicensed or non-registered transfer systems – is deemed to be declining, it is still estimated to account for 15 to 20 per cent of all migrant remittances globally. While acknowledging that the term "hawala" does not have one universal definition, FATF officials used it as early as 1990 to describe any method of transferring money that exists outside of the formal banking system. These remittance systems have been stigmatized and accused of playing a role in widespread collusion with international terrorist networks, although no empirical evidence supported this claim so frequently disseminated by the media at the time. In 2008, Passas and Maimbo underlined that no use of hawala by Al-Qaida was found in the United States and only one case, then very recent, in Europe.[19] In a similar vein, the alarmist tone of the last FATF report on the role of hawala was in contrast with the lack of known transgressions, as noted several times by the authors of the report themselves.[20] With these remarks, it would be naïve and erroneous to fall into the opposite trap that consists in presenting an ideal-type of informal remittance system as necessarily virtuous. No system is "naturally" immune from criminal activities. Like the banking system, hawala-type systems can be abused, especially in areas where they play a critical role, including in Afghanistan and Pakistan.[21] But to make the jump to insist on a particular and preferential connection between flows of illicit money and informal hawala money transfer systems is another thing; especially when the sudden closures of such remittance services in the name of counter-terrorism have immediate detrimental consequences for large populations, such as in Somalia with the controversial US shut-down of Al-Barakaat in November 2001.[22] Several arguments have been put forward to try to understand this stigmatization, including lack of expertise,[23] cultural and economic imperialism,[24] as well as political issues of surveillance and traceability (being understood as the only way to regulate the contingent order).[25]

The securitization of informal remittance services has also been imputed to the banking industry. As the interpretation goes, major international banks would have seen the opportunity to eliminate the informal competition in the massive market of migrant remittances. Without being totally irrelevant, this interpretation should be at least refined and nuanced. Although there are cases of banking pressures against informal money remitters, similar cases also exist against money transfer operators with the de-risking phenomenon. Moreover, it is often hard to tell whether this situation is the result of an aggressive business attitude or simply the fear of regulators and state authorities. In 2006, Philip W. Milne, president and CEO of MoneyGram International:

> address[ed] in greater detail the bank discontinuance issue, which is continuing to cause serious problems for many money services businesses, including MoneyGram and its agents. The problem is one in which banks are either closing the accounts of existing money services businesses, or refusing to open new accounts for them. The businesses are being told by banks, some of which they have had relationships with for years, that the business must choose between closing their account or ceasing to offer any kind of MSB [money service business] services. When they ask their bankers "why?" they are frequently told that the bank's regulator considers money services businesses to be high-risk and the regulator advises the bank to avoid doing business with such entities.[26]

This situation is akin to Naylor's argument pointing out that, ironically enough, it is by wanting to protect themselves from the state and related-supervisory authorities rather than from criminals that banks might finally go too far, for fear of sanctions as well as legal, reputational and financial damage.[27]

In addition to the emphasis placed on informal remittance services, the entire remittance industry has been impacted. As a result of national and international norms on money laundering and terrorist financing, guidelines issued by regulators has included a list of potentially high-risk clients and industries containing, among others, foreign residents and non-residents, and money services businesses.[28] Since then, the business model of money transfer operators has been perceived as "inherently high risk" in relation to dirty money, although this risk assessment is in contrast with the low number of identified legal violations.[29] By placing money transfer operators in the "high-risk client" category, and therefore under strict surveillance, financial regulators have generated an aura of uncertainty and unease around these businesses, with banks adopting risk-avoidance strategies.

Migrant remittances in face of de-risking phenomenon

The fact that JP Morgan Chase followed by Bank of America had been threatened with lawsuits for having held money services businesses accounts suspected of money laundering added another factor in the overall concern. Starting in 2006, Bank of America closed all of its money services businesses accounts indiscriminately. Western Union, Money-Gram and many other institutions also followed suit.[30] Banking supervisory authorities tried, but failed, to fix the problem by claiming that this remittance industry as a whole was not an unacceptable risk. The vast majority of banks continued to consider that the safest option was still to close these accounts.[31] Thus, 90 per cent of banks in the United States refused to have money services businesses as clients.[32] As a result, the latter had to focus on the remaining 10 per cent. Often, their new banks, despite being accommodating, were located hundreds of kilometres away, sometimes even in another state, leading to additional costs for the money services businesses. While the pressure placed on remittance systems post-2001 has encouraged banks to enter the migrant remittance market, this same force has also, and more importantly, helped strike fear into a number of institutions concerned with the "risks" associated with this market.

> The business is usually pretty good when they do see something that looks to be … beyond their risk appetite. Then they will demarket the client. They don't want to take on any regulatory risk. Demarket is basically our exit, all the accounts are closed.[33]

The significant trend of de-risking within major banks has grown over the past years across the financial industry and beyond the US. In 2013, Barclays already contacted 140 UK-based remittance businesses about the closure of their accounts.[34] In 2016, Artingstall *et al.* indicated that two UK banks were together closing about 1600 accounts per month in the name of their risk-appetite, including 1000 personal accounts and 600 business accounts.[35] More generally, among the money transfer operators who completed the World Bank survey in 2015, a significant part declared that they can no longer access banking services.[36]

De-risking strategies are thus partly enforced on the basis of business sector assessment. Financial institutions have chosen to limit relationships or even to stop doing business with money transfer operators because remittance sectors are officially considered very high-risk or "too risky". The impulse comes from big banks but their decision "may cause a 'cascade effect' of excessive caution based around a reasonable fear by the smaller banks that their own relationships with larger ones will be imperilled should they bank these sectors".[37] In this regard, "rich country banks increasingly report withdrawing correspondent banking services from banks in high risk jurisdictions, including many poor countries, reducing their access to the global financial system".[38]

More generally, in accordance with the risk-based approach on money laundering and terrorist financing, the intensity, frequency and ultimately the cost of surveillance and compliance obligations are proportionate to the level of risk.[39]

> We look at it from a risk tolerance perspective. Can we mitigate the risk enough to keep the risk at a low level with that customer and how much does it cost for us to mitigate that risk? The cost of monitoring for some customers, for some groups of customers, it is just not making sense for us to keep them in. MSBs [money services businesses] for instance. The amount of time that cost to monitor them is … And generally the high balance customers, they just have one [financial] product with us. They are not really bringing a lot of revenue into the organisation and so the cost–benefit does not deliver. It costs us more to mitigate the risk of those customers than the benefits that we are getting from them. So ….[40]

The higher the risk, the higher the costs are for accounts and transactions monitoring practices in order for banks to be compliant with legal obligations. It becomes a cost–benefit story in which the small and medium-sized remittance businesses are more likely to be excluded than the biggest money transfer operators, with a distortion of competition and an increasing concentration of market share.[41]

> [R]egulators sometimes send mixed signals about whether and how banks and other entities should manage their ML/TF [money laundering/terrorist financing] risk, which sometimes results in simplistic risk assessment methodologies being applied by these entities. There may also be a chilling effect resulting from the imposition of legitimate fines on some large banks for egregious contraventions of anti-money laundering, counter the financing of terror and, particularly, sanctions laws (commonly referred to collectively as AML/CFT). These factors, along with others, have led banks to adopt an understandably conservative position. This includes exiting from providing services to firms, market segments and countries that are seen as higher risk, lower profitability and could become the source of costly future fines, monitorships or even prosecutions. Banks are engaging in "de-risking" by

> ceasing to engage in types of activities that are seen to be higher risk in a wholesale fashion, rather than judging the risks of clients on a case-by-case basis. Individual banks may be acting rationally in not serving certain types of clients, due to a variety of factors. However, the implementation of AML/CFT appears to have created categories of clients whose business cannot justify the associated compliance costs. The financial exclusion of such clients creates yet another obstacle for poverty alleviation and economic growth, especially in poor countries.[42]

Conclusion

Ultimately, the securitization of migrant remittances may end up with a lose-lose relationship between the promoters of anti-money laundering and counter-terrorism financing and the promoters of the Sustainable Development Goals. If money transfer operators are pushed out of the main banks, they have to find alternatives that may be more expensive for them and their customers – starting with the low-skilled migrant workers and their relatives – and/or less transparent, with the unintended consequence of making the formal informal. International efforts against crimes and international efforts against poverty and inequalities across the globe are thus inter-related, and both threatened under the present circumstances.

Notes

1 UN Sustainable Development Goal 10.C – Reduce Inequality within and among Countries.
2 World Bank, "About Remittance Prices Worldwide. Making Markets More Transparent" (Washington DC 2017).
3 World Bank Group, "Migration and Remittances Factbook 2016" (Washington DC 2017).
4 IFAD, *Sending Money Home: Contributing to the SDGs, One Family at a Time* (The International Fund for Agricultural Development 2017: 7).
5 Ibid.
6 World Bank, "About Remittance Prices Worldwide. Making Markets More Transparent" (Washington DC 2017).
7 UN, "Progress of Goal 10 in 2017. Sustainable Development Knowledge Platform" (New York 2017).
8 World Bank, "An Analysis of Trends in Cost of Remittance Services". *Remittance Prices Worldwide*, Issue 23 (2017).
9 Ibid.
10 World Bank Group and KNOMAD, "Migration and Remittances. Recent Developments and Outlook". *Migration and Development*, Brief 26 (2016).
11 IFAD, *Sending Money Home: Contributing to the SDGs, One Family at a Time* (The International Fund for Agricultural Development 2017).

12 Ibid.
13 World Bank, "Remittance Prices Worldwide. 5x5 Objective" (Washington DC 2017).
14 Cirasino, M., "Reducing the Costs of Transferring Remittances: How Realistic Is the Proposed Target for Post-2015?", 13th Coordination Meeting on International Migration, New York, 12–13 February 2015; UN Inter-Agency Task Force on Financing for Development. "Remittances – Issue Brief Series" (New York 2016); World Bank, "About Remittance Prices Worldwide. Making Markets More Transparent" (Washington DC 2017).
15 FATF, "FATF Takes Action to Tackle De-risking" (Paris 2017).
16 Durner, T. and Shetret, L., *Understanding Bank De-Risking and its Effects on Financial Inclusion*. Oxfam International, 2015; Lowery, C. (Chair), *Unintended Consequences of Anti-Money Laundering Policies for Poor Countries. A CDG Working Group Report*. Center for Global Development, 2015; World Bank, "Report on the G20 Survey on De-Risking Activities in the Remittance Market" (Washington DC 2015); Artingstall, D., Dove, N., Howell, J. and Levi, M., *Drivers and Impacts of De-risking*. A study of representative views and data in the UK, by John Howell & Co. Ltd. for the Financial Conduct Authority, 2016.
17 World Bank Group and KNOMAD, "Migration and Remittances. Recent Developments and Outlook". *Migration and Development*, Brief 26 (2016).
18 FATF, "The Role of Hawala and Other Similar Service Providers in Money Laundering and Terrorist Financing" (Paris 2013: 9).
19 Maimbo, S. M. and Passas, N., "The Design, Development and Implementation of Regulatory and Supervisory Frameworks for Informal Funds Transfer Systems", in T. Biersteker and S. Eckert, eds., *Countering the Financing of Terrorism* (Routledge, 2008: 179–182).
20 FATF, "The Role of Hawala and Other Similar Service Providers in Money Laundering and Terrorist Financing" (Paris 2013).
21 Roth, J., Greenburg, D. and Wille, S., *National Commission on Terrorist Attacks upon the United States: Monograph on Terrorist Financing* (National Commission on Terrorist Attacks upon the United States 2004); FATF, "The Role of Hawala and Other Similar Service Providers in Money Laundering and Terrorist Financing" (Paris 2013).
22 Razavy, M., "Hawala: An Underground Haven for Terrorists or Social Phenomenon?" *Crime, Law and Social Change*, 44, 3 (2005): 277–299; Vlcek, W., "Development vs. Terrorism: Money Transfers and EU Financial Regulations in the UK". *The British Journal of Politics and International Relations*, 10, 2 (2008): 286–302; Haggerty, K. and Razavy, M., "Hawala Under Scrutiny: Documentation, Surveillance and Trust". *International Political Sociology*, 3, 2 (2009): 139–155; Passas, N., "Fighting Terror with Error: The Counter-Productive Regulation of Informal Value Transfers". *Crime, Law & Social Change*, 45, 4–5 (2006): 315–336; de Goede, M., "Hawala Discourses and the War on Terrorist Finance". *Environment and Planning D: Society and Space*, 21 (2003): 513–532; De Goede, M., *Speculative Security: The Politics of Pursuing Terrorist Monies* (University of Minnesota Press, 2012).
23 Warde, I., *The Price of Fear: The Truth Behind the Financial War on Terror* (University of California Press 2007).
24 McCulloch, J. and Pickering, S., "Suppressing the Financing of Terrorism: Proliferating State Crime, Eroding Censure and Extending Neo-colonialism". *British Journal of Criminology*, 45 (2005): 470–486.

25 Amicelle, A. and Jaquet-Chiffelle, D.-O., “La traçabilité, une technique de stigmatisation? Retour sur la problématisation de l’hawala dans le contexte antiterroriste”. *Revue internationale de criminologie et de police technique et scientifique*, LXVIII, 3 (2015): 338–353.
26 United States House of Representatives, “Testimony by Philip W. Milne, President and CEO, MoneyGram International, Inc. Before the United States House of Representatives Financial Services Subcommittee on Financial Institutions and Consumer Credit: Hearing on Bank Secrecy Act’s Impact on Money Services Businesses” (Washington DC 2006: 16).
27 Naylor, R. T., *Wages of Crime: Black Markets, Illegal Finance, and the Underworld Economy* (Cornell University Press 2004).
28 National Money Transmitter’s Association, “Personal Communication from D. Landsman, Executive Director. November 2006. Bank Secrecy Act Anti-Money Laundering Examination Manual”. *Appendix J: Quantity of Risk Matrix*, 2006.
29 World Bank, “Report on the G20 Survey on De-Risking Activities in the Remittance Market” (Washington DC 2015).
30 Bester, H., “Implementing FATF Standards in Developing Countries and Financial Inclusion: Findings and Guidelines”. Genesis, Final report, 2008.
31 Federal Banking Agencies, “Joint Statement on Providing Banking Services to Money Services Businesses Issued by the Federal Banking Agencies” (Washington 30 March 2005).
32 Bester, H., “Implementing FATF Standards in Developing Countries and Financial Inclusion: Findings and Guidelines”. Genesis, Final report, 2008.
33 Interview with a bank compliance officer, Canada, 2015.
34 Lowery, C. (Chair), *Unintended Consequences of Anti-Money Laundering Policies for Poor Countries. A CDG Working Group Report*. Center for Global Development, 2015.
35 Artingstall, D., Dove, N., Howell, J. and Levi, M., *Drivers and Impacts of Derisking*. A study of representative views and data in the UK, by John Howell & Co. Ltd. for the Financial Conduct Authority, 2016.
36 World Bank, “Report on the G20 Survey on De-Risking Activities in the Remittance Market” (Washington DC 2015).
37 Artingstall, D., Dove, N., Howell, J. and Levi, M., *Drivers and Impacts of Derisking*. A study of representative views and data in the UK, by John Howell & Co. Ltd. for the Financial Conduct Authority, 2016.
38 Lowery, C. (Chair), *Unintended Consequences of Anti-Money Laundering Policies for Poor Countries. A CDG Working Group Report*. Center for Global Development, 2015.
39 Amicelle, A. and Iafolla, V., “Suspicion-in-the-Making: Surveillance and Denunciation in Financial Policing”. *The British Journal of Criminology*. Published 07 September 2017.
40 Interview with a bank compliance officer, Canada, 2015.
41 Ibid.; IFAD, *Sending Money Home: Contributing to the SDGs, One Family at a Time* (The International Fund for Agricultural Development 2017).
42 Lowery, C. (Chair), *Unintended Consequences of Anti-Money Laundering Policies for Poor Countries. A CDG Working Group Report*. Center for Global Development, 2015.

14 Gan's journey from Thailand

Gan and Yewa S. Holiday

Gan and Yewa have been friends for over 25 years since they met through Gan's partner, George. Gan is the youngest of five brothers and sisters. He migrated from Thailand to Saudi Arabia and the UK to support his family. A fall which occurred while working in Saudi Arabia has, over the years, undermined his ability to continue the one thing he loves doing – working.

GAN: To begin with, my family ran a private primary school in Singburi, Thailand. My father was a head teacher and helped my oldest sister run the school. Before I finished school, the government changed the education system so a lot of private schools couldn't survive and closed down. We had to sell our school to the bigger school next door. After school, I wanted to go to work straightaway because of the family's financial crisis. My brother has three children but wasn't working. I didn't go to university or college because I looked for a job to help my family.

There was no permanent work. I worked in restaurants in Bangkok for a while, until I turned twenty when I had to do military service. After I left the Army, I thought, *What next? What can I do?* At the time, people who wanted to make money went to work in the Middle East.[1]

One of my brother's friends ran an agency so we contacted him and paid the 10,000 baht fee.[2] The agency sent me to work in Saudi Arabia for an Arabic company.[3]

I started to work … as a carpenter – [chuckles] – I have no knowledge of – [laughs] – carpentry at all! We worked 8 to 5 with an hour for lunch. We had to live and sleep where we were building – on the construction site. The conditions were difficult and unhygienic. People from the company cooked lunch which was free but they cooked in dirty conditions. We had to wash our clothes with our hands. The loos were basic and the showers were in a wooden shed – it was just awful!

Anyway, after working for a month, the company wanted an office assistant who could speak a little English. I thought – *oh why not? I can type. I can speak English, even though not completely fluent* … I just wanted a better job. I got the job. For the first two months we got money, but then there was no money.

…So we hung on because you can't strike in Saudi Arabia. What we did is – someone advised us – *you go to work but you don't need to do any work. Just sit there. But you can't just strike! You go to the site but just hang around there without working…*

Everybody did that. And the company started to fold. Someone contacted the Thai Embassy, because lots of Thai people were working there (there were also people from the Philippines and Sri Lanka). They contacted construction companies, Japanese, Arabic and other companies – they advertised in newspapers and radio for companies to take people. A Japanese company – Hazama – picked me and some others up.[4]

I worked for the new company for two years, first in the north, then Jeddah in the south. In the second year, the company moved me to Riyadh. I had a job and money. Daily life was 8 to 5 with a lunch break. Every day a coach picked us up to go to the site and we worked until midday. At lunchtime, a coach drove us back to the complex where we lived. After lunch, we worked from 1 to 5. The complex had a swimming pool, tennis court, our rooms were cleaned. There was a laundry and restaurant on site. It was perfect. Once a week, there was a coach trip to the sea or a shopping centre. Labourers lived in 12 bed dormitories. Foremen and supervisors shared rooms with one person. I shared with my Thai supervisor.

My job was Camp Assistant doing paperwork in the office. But I began as a Foreman Manager. That's when I had the accident. I fell off the top of a two-storey building.

We were working with concrete. The concrete ran too quickly and then the pipe started to shake – it couldn't hold the concrete and the five of us fell off the scaffolding. Fortunately, the ground was sand.[5]

At the time I didn't have a problem. You just carry on working afterwards because there's nothing damaged, you think. *Are you fine?* Everybody just stood up and looked fine – [laughs] to them! So we carry on working.

The Japanese company is quite good about health and safety, it was okay if anybody was sick, you had to wear a helmet and everything is quite safe.[6]

I worked there for two and a half years. Every year we had a month's holiday. The company paid for everything. The third year when I returned, the economy had changed. The company had to make cuts. Instead of $15,000 a year, you got maybe $8000 a year.[7]

And I said to myself, *I don't want to do this*. I contacted one of my father's former students who used to study at our school who lived in the UK. He was the owner of the Philbeach Hotel, the gay hotel in Earls Court, London.[8]

Gan went to the UK where he studied English and worked at the Philbeach as a chambermaid. He later worked in a number of Thai restaurants where he earned about £12,000 after tax and sent 90 per cent of his earnings to his family in Thailand. During this time, his back worsened.

GAN: Well, I feel like my back is kind of like come and go but it wasn't that bad at all. I'd still be able to do things. Every now and then you feel numb on your legs for maybe five minutes, then it would disappear. It took ten, twenty years before it got bad.

I didn't go to a doctor. I didn't think about my health. I was always thinking, *how can I make money for my family?*

The last place I worked was the Thai Pot near Covent Garden. I started to feel numb in my legs. And pain down through my left leg. And I couldn't stand longer than ten minutes. I had to sit down. And I thought, *this isn't good*. But I carried on working for almost six months until when I started to walk, I had to stop and sit down because of the pain. I had to drag my leg along. I phoned my mum. And my mum said, *well you have to have an operation…*

I went to the doctor but he just said there was nothing wrong with me … That's why I decided to phone my mum.

I went to Thailand. Within a month after the MRI scan, the doctor there said the disc between the bone and my back is cracked and pressing on the nerve because of the fall in Saudi Arabia … and so I have to have a laminectomy. It cost £15,000. They put in metal to support the bone. Before the operation, the doctor told me 95 per cent of people who had the operation would lead a normal life. The other 5 per cent might end up with chronic back pain. So I said, *well, I'd better do something…*

YEWA: …take that risk…

GAN: …yeah … *take that risk*. And, yes, afterwards, that's what happened.

YEWA: You were in the 5 per cent.

GAN: Yes. I came back here after a month in Thailand and a few days later, I was working.[9] I worked for two months. My back went bad again. I couldn't stand longer than five minutes. So I stopped working and went back to the GP. He said, *there's nothing serious. You can't just turn up like this, you have to make an appointment.* I was so angry. I just left and started to cry on the street with George. I said, *I don't want to go back to that doctor.*

...And we changed, we moved to a new clinic just across the street. The new doctor is an amazing doctor. He sent me to the ... pain management clinic ...

GEORGE: ... in the National Hospital for Neurology and Neurosurgery ...

GAN: I saw the hospital doctor there and he went through my medical history and said, *well, I think you have to learn to live with it. I think nothing we can do here now because people who have chronic back pain have to learn to live with the pain ...*

I went back to my GP. I said, *well, it's not good enough. Even though I learn how to live with it, the pain doesn't go away!* So the doctor gave me a Brutans patch ...[10] He said, *put the patch on your back, one patch a week, you can increase the patch, up to two patches a week.* I've been using this medication for over 12 years now. It's the only medication which works which helps me to ease the pain because other medication makes me feel sick but the pain doesn't go away! But this one even the side effect is still there but at least the pain is much better.

I can't work because of the pain – it makes me too unpredictable and unreliable. I thought if I can sort the pain out then I can go back to work. I had no other option but to take the patches.

About three years before I stopped working, I sent the family much less than I used to send. The children had finished university and started working so I was only supporting my mum. I could save a lot of money for myself.

When I came back after the back operation, I said to my mum, *look, I can't send you money any more because I can't work. I have no income now.* And she said, *we're fine now, you don't need to worry about that.* So, I stopped. I spent some money on the operation in Thailand, I came back here and lived off my savings. I've used all my savings now.

YEWA: You've talked about the operation, and losing your work. What other consequences ...

GAN: I lost my confidence. I don't like socialising. Because people are always talking about work. If they know me, *oh! Are you working yet?* If they don't know me, *oh! What's your job?* It's embarrassing because I feel I have no self-respect. I don't like the word 'unemployed' because I've been working all my life. And I like working. If

I meet someone, a stranger, I lie, *oh, I'm still working*. I don't like to mention about me being unable to work.

YEWA: What would you say are the positive things about your experience as an international labour migrant?

GAN: Helping my family go through the financial crisis and have a better life because they had a chance to go to university because of my money. My nephew and niece both work in big Thai companies and earn a lot of money. They travel and work abroad, but their base is in Thailand. They can fly abroad, work abroad and then return. So that's the positive thing, that I have helped people, my family, to have a better life.

YEWA: Yes, and I think that's quite a nice sort of ending really because at the beginning we were talking about how we were focussing on international low-skilled labour migration and the difficulties and the costs associated with that kind of migration as opposed to being a citizen or being a high-skilled labour migrant and the people you've helped in your family, you've helped them become these high skilled…

GAN: …high skilled … yes…

YEWA: …migrants who can fly around the world…

GAN: I think that's one thing I'm really proud of because … every time I look at them, I always think, *this is my job!* If I wasn't there with my sister, they wouldn't be able to do this kind of job and support their whole family now. They are still supporting the whole family group, whoever in the family has a problem, they still help each other without me having to say, *look, you can come to me*. But they know I don't earn anything now. So they say, *no, don't worry about us, we can support our family ourselves*. That's the positive thing.

Notes

1 Thai migration to the Gulf began in the 1970s, Ching-lung Tsay, 'Labor Migration and Regional Changes in East Asia' (2002) 40 Southeast Asian Studies 372; by 1990, 63 per cent of migrants in the Middle East (3.2 million) were Asian, mainly in Saudi Arabia (over 2 million), Ray Jureidini, 'Middle East Guestworkers' in Matthew J. Gibney and Randall Hansen (eds), *Immigration and Asylum from 1900 to the Present* (ABC-CLIO 2005) 405; Leon J. Warshaw, 'Precarious Employment and Child Labour' in Jeanne Mager Stellman (ed.), *Encyclopaedia of Occupational Health and Safety* (ILO 1998) 24.9; Ray Jureidini, '"Arab Gulf States: Recruitment of Asian Workers", Gulf Labor Markets and Migration' [2014] Migration Policy Centre (European University Institute) and Gulf Research Centre (Cambridge), GLMM – EN – No. 3/2014 www.grc.net/index.php?frm_module=contents&frm_action=detail_book&frm_type_id=&pub_type=11&publ_id=12&sec=Contents&frm_title=Research%20Papers&book_id=84451&op_lang=en&sec_type=h&publ_type=54.

2 About £250 in the 1980s.

3 Gan's migration coincided with the country's third phase of labour migration, Jureidini, 'Middle East Guestworkers' (n 1) 404–406. Gan is unable to recall the name of this company where he worked for only three months.

4 Hazama was established in 1889 initially working on railway, bridge and hydroelectric constructions. In 2003, it merged with the Ando Corporation to become Hazama Ando Corporation – see www.ad-hzm.co.jp/english/corporate/history.html.

5 Globally, the construction industry has the highest rate of accidents. In 2014, Mosly found that none out of 100 construction sites in Saudi Arabia provided safety harnesses to workers to protect them from falls. Stable and safely secured scaffolding was provided in 48.4 per cent of sites, Ibrahim Mosly, 'Safety Performance in the Construction Industry of Saudi Arabia' (2015) 4 International Journal of Construction Engineering and Management 238, 238–242.

6 Nevertheless, the fact of the accident and the lack of subsequent medical examination suggest a conflict with art 12(g) of the 1975 ILO MWC (equal treatment in working conditions for migrants). The 1990 MWC provides for equality of treatment in relation to health (art 25(a)) and access to medical care and safety in working conditions (art 28). This was not in force at the time of the accident. Neither has been ratified by Saudi Arabia.

7 Gan's migration coincided with lower growth rates in oil revenue compared to the early 1980s and 1990s, Ådne Cappelen and Robin Choudhury, *The Future of the Saudi Arabian Economy* (Statistics Norway 2000) 10–11.

8 Philbeach Hotel, which closed in 2008, was one of the largest gay hotels in Europe, 'Out and About', *Guardian* (London, 16 January 2005); Philbeach Hotel, www.lgbtarchive.uk/wiki/Philbeach_Hotel.

9 At this stage, Gan had indefinite leave to remain in the UK.

10 The patch is for round-the-clock treatment of moderate to severe chronic pain that cannot be otherwise controlled, Sanjay Bajaj, Abigail Whiteman and Brigitta Brandner, 'Transdermal Drug Delivery in Pain Management' (2011) 11 Continuing Education in Anaesthesia Critical Care & Pain 39, 42.

15 Then and now, here and there

Personal and academic perspectives on migration

Martin O. Heisler

Historians have often remarked that the history of humanity is that of migration; students of migration have cast it as a history of humanity. Migration is timeless and ubiquitous. In many respects, it differs from what it was even a few decades ago; and as diverse as migration to and in the West is, it is quite unlike migration in much of the rest of the world. It is imperative, therefore, to specify *when and where and whom* we are talking about, to put observations into temporal, spatial and societal context. In trying to draw insights from my experiences with, and study of, migration, three connected factors stand out: the prevailing *political and normative circumstances* and, at a micro level, the *social, economic, cultural and political capital* available to migrants. Each of these factors has changed markedly in the western world since the middle of the twentieth century, when my personal migration history began; those shifts are reflected in the premiums – economic, social and psychological – exacted from migrants, especially those perceived to offer few or limited skills useful for the host society. Both my personal experience and my research point to strong connections across those three dimensions.

From the personal to the professional

The study of the impact of migration on people and on societies has been one of my principal occupations for more than 40 years. But, although I am a migrant and married to an immigrant who has also written extensively about migration, the subject's attraction has been professional rather than personal. Not long after I began to teach and write about politics and international relations, it became evident that migration across the boundaries of states and cultures is vital for both the places of origin and destination; it often influences regional and even global relationships. Migration affects the dynamics of not only the economies of both sending and receiving countries but also their societies and polities. Most importantly, it is central in the lives of migrants and their families.

Many of the connections between migration and the vitality – perhaps even the stability and viability – of societies became apparent in the wake of the OPEC oil embargo following the 1973 Arab-Israeli war.[1] The embargo and its economic consequences in several western and central European countries drew attention to the presence of people who were seen as temporary "guest workers". Since I studied the politics and international relations of Europe, it was in that realm that I first became attentive to this issue.[2] While neither the oil embargo nor foreign workers per se constituted a threat to the security of European host societies, awareness that a changing energy landscape could introduce great uncertainties into their economies problematized the presence of large numbers of migrants and raised questions about the possibility of repatriating them.

Such concerns fostered the development of modern migration studies in Europe and of a *problématique* centred on the host societies.[3] Given my interests in comparative and world politics, however, my attention was drawn to foreign workers' places of origin as well. If the newly recognized issues were of modest importance in the West, the prospect of the repatriation of migrant workers was of great concern for the sending countries. Given their relatively weak economies, social services and infrastructures and surplus of newly urbanized un- or under-employed working age men, the sudden return of many of their citizens would strain the capacity of labour markets to absorb them. That, in turn, would raise the risks of political and social instability. The interconnectedness of population movements, vast differences in patterns of migration around the world, and the often precarious circumstances of many migrants led me to think in broadly comparative-historical terms, with an unwavering focus on people.[4]

The introspection that comes with age uncovered links between my personal history and insights from my research. The personal consists of my experiences; the professional alludes to patterns in migration and in the lives of the migrants I studied and the literatures with which I have become familiar. Those patterns are shaped by fluid economic and political circumstances, not only in the host and sending societies but around the world and by shifting legal regimes and, crucially, evolving norms.

From child refugee to working immigrant

My father and I escaped from Hungary to the British zone of occupation in Austria in early 1949, a few months after Hungary's newly consolidated communist regime closed its borders to all emigration. We were smuggled across a heavily mined field by a "coyote", on a moonless night, beneath several rows of barbed wire and under the klieg lights of snipers in guard towers. Thus, at the age of 11, I became a political refugee, a stateless person, a trans-migrant in Austria and later in Paris. After a year in Paris, I immigrated (legally) to the United States. Much later, as an adult in a privileged position, I emigrated from the United States to Denmark and, after a few years, returned to the United States, where I had retained citizenship. During the last 50 years, I have lived and worked in many countries for various periods, moving across borders legally and without difficulty.

As a child migrant, I was somewhat aware of some of the economic dimensions of the migrant premium. My material circumstances were extremely poor when I was a refugee in Austria and France and for some time after arriving in the United States. I depended on support from charitable organizations (which, by the late 1940s and early 1950s, had largely exhausted their resources) and occasionally on the parents of schoolmates. I was never entirely without shelter or food, but I was acutely aware of the psychological and social costs of penury and dependence. These included having to cope without a family or other adults to whom I was personally connected; living and going to school in languages I initially did not understand; adjusting to different cultures and circumstances in rapid succession; and, for a year, uncertainty regarding the future – when or even whether I could rejoin my father, my surviving parent.[5] Being without resources left me dependent and relatively isolated; it set me apart and reinforced the linguistic and cultural barriers between me and people with whom I came in contact.[6]

From my arrival in the United States, in August 1950, until I finished university I always worked in part-time or temporary jobs, initially selling newspapers on a street corner, then delivering them by bicycle; washing dishes in a restaurant; washing cars; selling ice cream; installing telephones; assembling machinery in a factory; clerking in a mail-room; cleaning offices. All of these jobs were at or near the bottom of the economic and social ladder. As a minor, I often worked longer than legally permitted for school children and I earned much less than the mandated minimum wage for adults. Sometimes I was paid less than the agreed wage or not paid at all, and if I complained I was dismissed. Once I reached the age of 18, I did receive the minimum wage, but had no job security until I settled into my profession, several years later. These experiences helped me to understand the circumstances of the low-skilled workers – documented or not – I came to know well over the years.

Much later I was living in Paris again, but this time in a privileged position as a "senior international research fellow" of the *Centre national de la recherche scientifique* (CNRS). There was no trace of the economic, psychological or social premiums exacted during my Parisian sojourn as a child. The difficulties I encountered were relatively trivial: finding a place to live; registering with the local police bureau and showing my visa and work permit; opening a bank account; navigating the French bureaucracy – mundane tasks confronting natives as well as immigrants. The fellowship allowed beginning a long-term undertaking: studying the roles of formal and social institutions in the integration or adaptation of immigrants in France – specifically, immigrants from North and West Africa and, as a "control group", Portugal.[7] It was such research that led me to truly appreciate the migrant premium – psychological and social, not only financial – imposed on the relatively low-skill workers I studied and the differences their legal status made in that premium and in their opportunities to establish ties in both migrant and native communities.

As a child part-time worker in America, I lacked the legal protections accorded most adult citizens or documented immigrants; laws designed to protect young workers were often ignored. The circumstances of the migrants with whom I worked in France – particularly those without formal residence or work permits – mirrored my early experiences. They, like most undocumented and some documented migrants in the American labour market, were often exploited, made to work under unsafe and illegal conditions and victimized by wage theft.[8] The problem was not the absence of legislation to prevent wage theft but the lack or inconsistency of enforcement.[9]

Change and persistence in the migrant premium

The social and psychological stress that accompanies migrants in low-skilled positions compounds the economic premium exacted from them. Regardless of their residence status, they are more vulnerable to wage theft than native workers. And they often lack the social and cultural capital and political resources to remonstrate on their own behalf – especially, as is the case in much of the world, if that would raise the risk of losing their employment. During my first five or six years in the United States, there were no adults who could protest or argue on my behalf. Even if my father could have taken time from his job, also near the bottom of the economic ladder, his command of English was not sufficient for the task; nor could he take time from work to remonstrate on my behalf without fear of being terminated. Low-wage migrants have few resources to defend their rights without the intercession of others.

There have been important changes in this regard in the last 40 or 50 years in most western and some central European countries and in the United States, though not in many other parts of the world. In the West, international norms and national legislation have mitigated some of the economic disadvantages migrants confronted in the past. But perhaps more has been achieved by a broad – amorphous may be the most appropriate adjective – variety of actors. Religion-based ("faith-based", in American parlance) and charitable organizations (foundations), civic or social associations have come to concern themselves with migrants' fundamental rights. With great variation from country to country, trade unions in Europe and the United States – with, admittedly, diminished political resources – have sought to protect the employment rights of migrant workers.[10] The provision of at least minimal health care for migrant workers and their families has become effectively organized in several regions of the United States, where access to public insurance for some documented and all undocumented workers is problematic.[11] Campaigns against wage theft are becoming increasingly effective.

Are conditions for migrant workers better or worse now than in the middle of the twentieth century, when I arrived in the United States? They are both better and worse, depending on the places and the particular circumstances of migration. One of my long-standing concerns in studying migration is that many theoretical frameworks and systematic data collection seem to stop at the edge of the western world. It is, therefore, difficult to appreciate – and sometimes even to recognize – changes for the better. Juxtaposed with the circumstances of, for instance, Zimbabwean (mostly undocumented or irregular) migrants in the Republic of South Africa or Filipina domestic servants in the United Arab Emirates, the economic premium paid by migrant workers in Europe and North America is not only of a different magnitude but perhaps of an essentially different character. The concern in the West centres on rights – economic, social, cultural and political. In many other parts of the world, migrant workers' circumstances range between the edge of survival and indentured status and effectively unregulated servitude.[12]

My argument is not that migrant workers in the West have no significant reasons for concern and legitimate demands; they do. The dual perspective of change over time and comparison with probably a majority of people living and working outside their countries of origin may help to uncover a progressive diminution of the fiscal dividend migrants in western countries must bear.

Notes

1 Although I wrote a research proposal at the time on the possible impacts of the oil crisis on foreign workers in Western Europe, it took several years to refocus my research programme on migration. An immediate consequence of the redirection of my thinking was to encourage doctoral students at the University of

Maryland to pursue the subject. The first to do so was Demetrios Papademetriou, who went on to co-found and serve as president of the Migration Policy Institute.

2 See, e.g., M. O. Heisler, "Transnational Migration as a Small Window on the Diminished Autonomy of the Modern Democratic State", *Annals of the Academy of Political and Social Science*, 485 (May 1986): 153–166; M. O. Heisler and B. S. Heisler, "Citizenship – Old, New, and Changing: Inclusion, Exclusion, and Limbo for Ethnic Groups and Migrants in the Modern Democratic State", in J. Fijalkovski, H. Merken and F. Schmidt, eds., *Dominant National Cultures and Ethnic Identities* (Berlin: Free University of Berlin, 1990), 91–128; M. O. Heisler, "Migration, International Relations and the New Europe: Theoretical Perspectives from Institutional Political Sociology", *International Migration Review* 26, 2 (Summer 1992): 596–622; M. O. Heisler and Zig Layton-Henry, "Migration and the Link Between Social and Societal Security", in Ole Wæver, Barry Buzan, Morten Kelstrup and Pierre Lemaitre, *Identity, Migration and the New Security Agenda in Europe* (London: Pinter, 1993).

3 That development can be dated from the publication, in 1973, of Stephen Castles and Godula Kosack, *Immigrant Workers and Class Structure in Western Europe* (Oxford and London: Oxford University Press).

4 See, for instance, M. O. Heisler, "Contextualizing Global Migration: Sketching the Socio-Political Landscape in Europe", *UCLA Journal of International Law and Foreign Affairs* 3, 2 (Fall/Winter 1998–99): 557–593; "Now and Then, Here and There: Migration and the Transformation of Identities, Borders and Orders", in M. Albert, D. Jacobson and Y. Lapid, eds., *Identities, Borders, Orders: Rethinking International Relations Theory* (Minneapolis and London: University of Minnesota Press, 2001), 225–247; and "Our Stories, Our Selves: Identities and the Dialogics of Narrative", in Michael Böll, ed., *Narrating Peoplehood amidst Diversity: Historical and Theoretical Perspectives* (Aarhus, DK: Aarhus University Press, 2011).

5 These conditions are, of course, common to refugees in virtually any place or time. I was still waiting for an entry visa my father was trying to obtain for me when the school year ended at the school in Paris where I had been given a place; he had arrived at his destination in the United States some months earlier. The outbreak of the Korean War in the summer of 1950 had halted the granting of entry visas for refugees.

6 While my sense of isolation was largely personal or individual, my research and that of others suggests that when migrants find others with linguistic and cultural affinities, they may be isolated as a group from the host society but the psychological isolation is mitigated.

7 The project funded by CNRS was "The Normative and Institutional Construction of Identity".

8 See, e.g., Elizabeth Fussell, "The Deportation Threat Dynamic and Victimization of Latino Migrants: Wage Theft and Robbery", *Sociological Quarterly* 52, 4 (Fall 2011): 593–615.

9 See, for instance, Nantiya Ruan, "Facilitating Wage Theft: How Courts Use Procedural Rules to Undermine Substantive Rights of Low-Wage Workers", 63 *Vanderbilt Law Review* 727 (2010).

10 See, e.g., Stefania Marino, "Trade Union Inclusion of Migrant and Ethnic Minority Workers: Comparing Italy and the Netherlands", *European Journal*

of Industrial Relations 18, 1 (March 2012): 5–20; Ruth Milkman, *L.A. Story: Immigrant Workers and the Future of the US Labor Movement* (New York: Russell Sage Foundation, 2006); John Wrench, "Trade Union Response to Immigrants and Ethnic Inequality in Denmark and the UK: The Context of Consensus and Conflict", *European Journal of Industrial Relations*, 10, 1 (March 2004): 7–30; Rinus Penninx and Judith Roosblad, eds., *Trade Unions, Immigration and Immigrants in Europe, 1960–1993* (New York and Oxford: Berghahn Books, 2000).

11 An exemplar of such an organization (it would be termed a charity in Britain) in the Pacific Northwest in the United States (where I live) is Virginia Garcia, a complex of comprehensive medical centres named after the young daughter of migrant farm workers who died from a simple infection because she and people like her had no access to medical care. Such organizations for the delivery of health care, including, increasingly, mental health services, exist in several countries and some transnational efforts to aid migrant workers in South America are being developed.

12 See, e.g., Jeffrey D. Pugh, "Negotiating Identity and Belonging through the Invisibility Bargain: Colombian Forced Migrants in Ecuador", *International Migration Review* (forthcoming 2017 – early view online); but cf. Claire Adida, *Immigrant Exclusion and Insecurity in Africa* (New York: Cambridge University Press, 2014). Also see Alexander Betts, *Survival Migration: Failed Governance and the Crisis of Displacement* (Ithaca and London: Cornell University Press, 2013).

Index